# POCKET NEIGHBORHOODS

ROSS CHAPIN Foreword by SARAH SUSANKA, author of *The Not So Big House*

# POCKET NEIGHBORHOODS

CREATING **SMALL-SCALE COMMUNITY** IN A **LARGE-SCALE WORLD**

**The Taunton Press**
Inspiration for hands-on living®

63 South Main Street, PO Box 5506, Newtown, CT 06470-5506

e-mail: tp@taunton.com

Editor: PETER CHAPMAN

Copy Editor: SETH REICHGOTT

Indexer: JIM CURTIS

Jacket and Interior design: ERICA HEITMAN-FORD for MUCCA DESIGN

Layout: HANA NAKAMURA and JEAN-MARC TROADEC for MUCCA DESIGN

Illustrators: ROSS CHAPIN, MARTHA GARSTANG HILL

The following names/manufacturers appearing in *Pocket Neighborhoods* are trademarks:
Medite®

Library of Congress Cataloging-in-Publication Data

Chapin, Ross.

  Pocket neighborhoods : creating small-scale community in a large-scale world / author, Ross Chapin ; foreword by Sarah Susanka.

    p. cm.

  Includes index.

  ISBN 978-1-60085-107-0

  1.  Neighborhood planning--United States. 2.  Community development--United States.  I. Title.

  HT167.C454 2011

  307.3'3620973--dc22

                          2010040242

Printed in China

10 9 8 7 6 5 4 3 2

*For Deborah, my wife, who saw the writer in me from Day One and helped me develop clear threads of thought; and for Aleah, our daughter, whose natural sense of authenticity helped me "see" what is "real."*

## ACKNOWLEDGMENTS

Several years ago, publisher Jim Childs and senior editor Peter Chapman came to visit me on Whidbey Island and approached me about writing a book. I suggested pocket neighborhoods as a topic, but at the time I was in the midst of developing our first communities and hardly had time to write. But the seed of the idea was germinated, and it would lay waiting for its time to unfold. I will be ever grateful to Peter for his belief in the idea. His steady patience, clarity, and guidance carried us through the long process of creation. I've enjoyed every moment of our teamwork and friendship.

When author Sarah Susanka saw my first pocket neighborhood, she understood it as an extension of the ideas she was writing about—"not so big" houses fitting into a larger fabric of community. Sarah has the ability to read the pulse of the culture through her public speaking engagements, and she conveyed to Taunton her belief that it was the right time for this book to be published.

On the home front, my wife and creative partner, Deborah, engaged in daily kitchen-table discussions and feedback to refine these ideas and offered her editorial eye as the work progressed.

I am filled with appreciation for all the assistance I've received along the way to bring this book into existence: to Jason Miller for helping get the book on its feet and for coming up with the inspired subtitle that clarified its focus; to Ken Gutmaker for his photographic eye for composition and detail; to friends and colleagues Lianna Clare Gilman, Vicki Robin, Mike Dunn, Nancy Pascoe, Steve Mouzon, Chuck Durrett, Grace Kim, and Michael Mehaffy for their insights; to Dan Burden for his enthusiastic encouragement; and to the many people who opened their homes and communities to me and shared their experiences.

The whole vision of pocket neighborhoods was made real through the rare design and development partnership I've had with Jim Soules. He was the spark that brought potentials together, and the engine that moved them forward. He drew me in with his fearlessness to look ahead with a sharp eye, trusting a gut sense for the right course, even when the prevailing voices in the industry were so cautious. We did good work. And through it all, I value his friendship.

Our neighborhood projects would not have been successful without collaboration with many people: Linda Pruitt tracked the financial details that allowed us to make realistic design decisions, led the marketing and sales efforts, and engaged her own uncanny sense of beauty with landscape and interior design. I am truly grateful for the organizational skills and steadfast support of my associate Karen DeLucas, who managed architectural details as well as communications through the flurry of creation. And no innovative project could find the light of day if not for the involvement of forward-thinking individuals at every step: pro-active city planners, bankers understanding the vision, craftsman-builders taking pride in their work, and buyers willing to live their values.

In the process of researching this book I have come to realize how much my own work is part of a long lineage of design and building, by people known and unknown. I am indebted to them all. The writings and built works of Christopher Alexander stand out as a perennial source of inspiration for me, ever since stumbling across his working manuscript of *A Pattern Language* in the mid-1970s. I hope that this book adds a humble thread to the conversation, and an inspiration to others in making a more whole and healthy world.

# TABLE OF CONTENTS

# FOREWORD

Have you ever wondered why the vast majority of neighborhoods in American towns and cities are missing a true sense of community? Residents share the place in name, and they pass each other in their cars each day as they come and go, but there's little real interaction. Many people today are wishing it were different, wishing that they could be part of a more supportive and neighborly community while still maintaining the sense of privacy they prize once within their home's walls.

When I was lamenting this lack of community with my old friend and fellow architect Ross Chapin, he painted an interesting analogy for me. He told me that he was recently at a garden party with twenty people sitting at a long table. At one point in the gathering, the guests took turns introducing themselves to the group at large. When Ross told them about his new book, someone asked, "What is a pocket neighborhood?" He pointed out that there had been three conversations going on at the table prior to the introductions: one at each end, and one in the middle. These are like three pocket neighborhoods along a block. Conversations pick up naturally in these smaller groups, while a conversation within the larger group requires organization. That said, imagine the guests turning their chairs away from the table and looking outward. All conversations would cease.

Carrying this analogy to many present-day neighborhoods, the front facades of the houses and garage doors may be facing the street, but the life inside the houses is oriented to the backyards. Residents have privacy, but any conversation among neighbors is difficult. The key to a successful pocket neighborhood is balancing privacy and community. Homes can have privacy while opening to a common space shared with a cluster of surrounding neighbors. Then, like friends around a dinner table, conversation is effortless.

There are, in fact, many spontaneously occurring pocket neighborhoods across this country that have sprung up around a shared common space. The people who live in such places know they share something extraordinary, even when they don't understand the source of the neighborhood's uniqueness.

Ross has been studying these accidental pocket neighborhoods for the past few years, in order to bring into being a more planned version of the same serendipitous community. His own version of the pocket neighborhood is a cluster of compact but beautifully designed homes, usually located within an existing small town or a well-established first-tier suburb. The key to the obvious success of these neighborhoods is that they are designed first and foremost for people rather than for automobiles.

With a centrally located green space or commons, in lieu of a street down the middle, and with a clearly and elegantly demarcated entrance into the neighborhood, a collective identity is created. Before long, neighbors get to know each other, just as the people at the garden party did, and provide for each other the kind of support system that family members across town, across state, or across country cannot. It is the opportunities for informal interactions that allow people to get to know their neighbors, and it is these interactions that provide the roots for true community to flourish.

Every few years a book comes along that profoundly shifts the way we think about a subject, and when we look back a decade or so after its publication, we see a dramatic shift brought about by the thoughts that book contains. I believe that the book you have in your hands right now is such a game changer. The model of community it describes provides a missing link in our longings for home, and a better place to live. My fervent hope is that it will provide people around the country with the vision and the inspiration to shape thriving pocket neighborhoods of their own. In my opinion this is the way to a vastly more livable and more sustainable future for our cities, for our towns, and most important, for ourselves.

*Sarah Susanka*
Raleigh, North Carolina
January, 2011

# Introduction

The home I grew up in was an American classic: a shingled bungalow in Minnesota with a wrap-around porch, within a neighborhood of homes built at the turn of the last century. My grandparents and great aunt lived on the next block, and our porch was the hub of lingering family conversations on warm summer evenings. The entire neighborhood was our playground, and I knew which houses I was welcomed into.

In the 1960s, the interstate freeway system extended out from St. Paul, opening the surrounding farmland to waves of suburban ranch homes. To my young eye, they were appallingly beige and plain. This mediocrity felt like an insult to the land, and I began imagining alternative designs for houses and neighborhoods that had more life and vitality. Looking back, I can see how these contrasts sparked my desire to become an architect.

I eased into a career as a young architect focused on designing individual homes fitted to the clients' particular needs and their sites. Yet no matter how well designed these homes may have been, I was left with the nagging feeling that I wasn't able to address the needs and desires of living in a community. Nearly all the neighborhoods I worked in were merely collections of individual houses, each an island to itself, with little real connection among neighbors. There was only so much I could do at the scale of one house.

At a talk I gave to a group of builders and architects, I met a developer who challenged me to think bigger. We decided to join forces and collaborate on building a cluster of small cottages that created a community together. They were tucked off of a busy street, like a pocket safely tucking away its possessions from the world outside. It seemed to me like a "pocket neighborhood," and the term stuck. The cottages had a very approachable style that everyone seemed to love. Yet beyond their appearance, it became immediately clear that we'd tapped into a deep, unmet longing for community. Soon after we completed our first pocket neighborhood (which we'll look at in detail in Chapter 6), word got out about them, and the response we received from across the country was electric. It was not just from small households or a particular age group, nor was it about the cottages themselves; what we heard was a widespread, deeply felt desire to live in a *real* neighborhood.

We continued to design and build variations of pocket neighborhoods to test the market for these small-scale communities. And during this time, I've sought to understand the key design principles that foster vibrancy and life in a community. In my explorations, I discovered a wide range of related projects, both historical and contemporary, that shed light on these principles. This book is an account of this search. My hope is that it will offer guideposts and inspiration to help restore the coherence of vibrant, small-scale communities in our large-scale world.

Facing page: My childhood home had a name that described what it was: "The Bungalow." From a child's perspective, it was part of a close-knit neighborhood of houses that we all felt to be part of "our world."

Below: Jim Soules and I jumped in to build a cluster of small cottages around a central landscaped green. We had to trust our hunches, as the project had no comparables, except for a similar cluster we had seen that was originally built in 1918.

7

"The cottages were tucked off of a busy street, like a pocket safely tucking away its possessions from the world outside. It seemed to me like a 'pocket neighborhood,' and the term stuck."

# DISCOVERING POCKET NEIGHBORHOODS

This book is about a pattern of settlement that is rare in America, yet common to traditional communities around the world. I call it a *pocket neighborhood*. By my definition, a pocket neighborhood is a cohesive cluster of homes gathered around some kind of common ground within a larger surrounding neighborhood. I like to think of it as a neighborhood within a neighborhood.

Pocket neighborhoods form at a scale where meaningful "neighborly" relationships are fostered—smaller than what we usually think of as a neighborhood, but larger than a couple of houses. Garden courts are good examples, but a pocket neighborhood could also be a coherent city block, a series of suburban houses with joined backyards, a reclaimed alley, "cohousing," or an elder housing cluster woven into a larger neighborhood.

Shared outdoor space is a key element of a pocket neighborhood. It is neither private (home, yard) nor public (a busy street, park), but rather a defined space between the private and public realms. The residents surrounding this common space share in its care and oversight, thereby enhancing a felt and actual sense of security and identity. Because of its location and design, the shared outdoor space fosters casual interaction among neighbors, which, in time, may grow into deeper, long-term friendships.

The Japanese phrase—*muko sangen ryo donari*—comes close to describing the scale of a pocket neighborhood. It translates as "three houses across and one to either side and back." These are one's immediate neighbors.

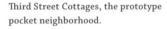

Third Street Cottages, the prototype pocket neighborhood.

8

Left: In a pocket neighborhood, a cluster of homes surrounds a shared commons.

Below: Shared outdoor space is a key element of a pocket neighborhood, whether in a rural, suburban, or urban location.

## WHAT'S THE RIGHT SIZE FOR A POCKET NEIGHBORHOOD?

A neighborhood might contain several hundred households, but when it comes to pocket neighborhoods, I believe the upper limit is in the range of 12 to 16 households. If a cluster has fewer than 4 households, it loses the sense of being a cluster, or a group. It lacks the clear sense of identity, diversity, or activity of a larger group.

On the other hand, when the number of households grows beyond a dozen or so, it becomes difficult for people to know their neighbors in any depth, or to live close enough to call on them in an emergency.

# WHAT IS A POCKET NEIGHBORHOOD?

Pocket neighborhoods are clustered groups of neighboring houses or apartments gathered around some sort of shared open space—a garden courtyard, a pedestrian street, joined backyards, or a reclaimed alley. They can be in urban, suburban, or rural areas.

A pocket neighborhood is a basic building block of a vibrant, healthy community.

A pocket neighborhood provides the setting for neighbors to develop meaningful relationships beyond the family. It is the physical basis for creating community with surrounding neighbors.

The shared commons of a pocket neighborhood is held and cared for by surrounding neighbors, who feel the space as an extension of their personal world.

In a pocket neighborhood, there is a collective sense of ownership that extends beyond the front yard gates to the edge of the shared commons at the street. A guest or stranger will feel this territorial sense as soon as they enter the commons.

Imagine you're 6 years old and your mom says "go out and play." If she's comfortable with you going beyond the front gate, you're likely living in a pocket neighborhood.

Pocket neighborhoods provide the basis for a sense of belonging and meaning—small-scale communities in a large-scale world.

A neighborhood is where you might describe "the red house on the corner of Elm and Main Street"—a known location, a kind of local landmark that helps define and give character to a neighborhood. But you may not know who lives there. In a pocket neighborhood, neighbors know one another: "Kate and Joey live across the way." These are neighbors you can ask about your child's earache or other daily dilemmas, and invite to join in an impromptu takeout order for pizza.

A pocket neighborhood is *not* the wider neighborhood of several hundred households, but a realm of a dozen or so neighbors who interact on a daily basis—like a neighborhood within a neighborhood.

# LIVING IN A LARGE-SCALE WORLD

Why pocket neighborhoods? Why now? The American Dream of owning a single-family home with a private yard and a garage seems to be what most people strive for. It is certainly what is being sold. Yet demographics and family structures have changed significantly since this version of the dream was awakened. We're living in a larger scale world than our grandparents, with more—or certainly different—stresses and pressures. Understanding how we arrived at where we are now will help us find ways to meet our deeper needs and desires.

## The Lure of Privacy

Houses are typically marketed on their virtues of curb appeal, size, privacy, and personal amenities. Realtors list an impressive two-story brick-faced portico, three-car garage, and a bathroom with every bedroom. A media room and backyard barbeque round out the amenities, making the home a self-reliant hub of family life.

Once new homeowners move in, however, it may take some time for them to meet their neighbors. The street out front is less likely to be a place to chat with a neighbor than a space to come and go through by car. Most activities happen in the privacy of the home and backyard, while the world beyond the front door is left vacant.

In many housing developments, the street is less likely to be a place to meet with neighbors than a space to come and go through by car. Family life is focused inside and in the walled backyard.

Looking at this in terms of scale, the small-scale levels of room, house, and backyard get a lot of attention, while the next-level scale of the street and block get little use. This means fewer opportunities to share a favorite recipe, tell about the trip to the lake, or discuss the upcoming mayor's election. Without daily relationships, nearby neighbors are less likely to call on one another to look after a child while going out for groceries, or check in on an elderly neighbor when the curtains haven't opened by 10 a.m. When this critical level of scale is weak or undefined, the vitality and resilience of a community are diminished.

## The Scale of Community and the American Dream

Let's face it: Humans are gregarious. We like to live around others. For thousands of years our ancestors lived in clusters, barrios, hamlets, neighborhoods, and villages. Many lived their whole lives within a small circle of where they were born.

For much of human history, walking distance defined the scale of community. Most of one's daily relationships in life took place, by circumstance, within an area defined by the distance a person could easily walk. Horses and wagons expanded the circle, but still, the scale of community was closely knit and tied to place. When Henry Ford took the Model T to the masses and a vast highway network unfurled across the American continent, proximity released its hold on close relationships, and the walk-circle community quietly disbanded. Work and friendships were just as likely to be found at distances measured in miles rather than blocks. Bell's telephone "miraculously" eliminated the bounds of distance all together. These technologies changed the scale of community as had never happened in all of history.

> "For much of human history, walking distance defined the scale of community."

The automobile and cheap, endless oil opened up "broad acres" of land, and a new American Dream took root, giving millions of people access to single-family home ownership. Fathers had well-paying work in the city, while mothers and children had a wholesome life in the suburbs. Or so the story goes.

## Stresses on the Family

Houses inched up in size over the years, even as family size diminished. And households became increasingly private and self-reliant. Subdivision developments were built hundreds of houses at a time. So-called neighborhoods were merely the byproduct of houses in close proximity. Unfortunately, development overshot the desire for privacy, leaving many people marooned on their own little islands in a sea of houses.

Evidence of isolation is clear. Grown children often settle in regions far from their parents. Young families, with little or no network of support, struggle with keeping up with mortgage or rental payments, commuting, arranging childcare, chauffeuring kids to after-school activities, monitoring Internet activity, shopping, preparing meals, and caring for a sick child. Families are not the only groups who are vulnerable. Some people find themselves single, by choice or circumstance, in the same predicament. Elderly people often face retirement alone, with limited resources or support networks. For many, the stress of being helpless in a large-scale world is overwhelming.

## Restoring Small-Scale Communities

Pocket neighborhoods can help mend the web of belonging, care, and support needed in a frayed world. Here, nearby neighbors can respond to daily needs in a way that friends across town and family across the country cannot. An elderly neighbor may need assistance trimming a hedge. Another neighbor needs help looking after the kids while going for a short errand, or feeding the cats while away on vacation. Impromptu encounters have neighbors chatting about the garden, the latest news, or reminiscing about old times. In time, these simple meetings may grow into caring relationships, offering friendship as well as support at a challenging time. These are the advantages of living in a small-scale community.

# PART ONE

# POCKET NEIGHBORHOOD PRECEDENTS

**The history of settlement is a fascinating story,** and one that continues to unfold as we work out our relationship with the automobile. Villages and towns nearly always had gathering places for the community—the village green, town square, market street, pub, church—that served the needs for economic, social, and religious exchange.

Sometimes, householders lived in clustered dwelling groups where their day-to-day needs were lightened by virtue of shared work and leisure: sharing the tasks of milling corn, making chapatis, washing clothes, tending children, as well as just sitting and talking, or gathering around the fire for stories. The commune of households made life easier and more enjoyable.

This type of clustered layout is rare today, as the single-family house on its own plot of ground has been the long-standing American Dream. Any talk about a "commune of households" is likely to be looked at with suspicion. We are, however, social animals, and a wide variety of prototypes have been created to meet the social and daily needs of small groups of householders—many of which could be regarded as pocket neighborhoods.

> "The house itself is of minor importance. Its relation to the community is the thing that really counts."
> —CLARENCE STEIN, PIONEER OF THE GARDEN CITY MOVEMENT

The historic pocket neighborhood precedents highlighted in this section date back to the 1400s, and came about through early initiatives for social security, by happenstance, by romantic reference to the old world, or by result of a grand vision. Whatever the reason, there is much to learn by studying their form and social life and applying it to our contemporary era.

## CHAPTER ONE

# Setting Up Camp

When community is the primary goal, human settlements form with a natural scale and order. Take, for example, the Methodist summer camp at Oak Bluffs on Martha's Vineyard. At its founding in 1835, members pitched tents in what was described as a "sweet disorder." Over many years of warm-weather gatherings, order and disorder alternated as tents clustered themselves around small parks and narrow lanes. Returning visitors began

Above: Oak Bluffs began as a summer campground of tents clustered around small parks and lanes.

Left: Today, "The Campground" swells with life as families come to spend the summer in their cottages.

replacing the tents with small wooden cottages with steeply pitched gables and ornamental moldings. Eventually, more than 300 cottages made up a community of pocket neighborhoods, which came alive with music and glowed with handmade lanterns at night.

Although the Oak Bluffs community was originally chartered to hold religious meetings, community life at "The Campground" today has a predominantly secular flavor. Neighbors gather for "community sings," with informal songs like "Waltzing Matilda" and "Good Night Eileen" filling the air between and above the cottages. A knitting group meets every Monday morning. There are ice cream socials, a children's parade, and "Illumination Night," when all the cottages are adorned with paper lanterns.

Sally Dagnall, a fifth-generation resident, remembers life as a child at The Campground. "When we came back every summer, it was like we never left our friends. We'd be in and out of each other's houses and roamed the neighborhood in packs. There were always a lot of relatives around, and kids listened in on the edges of the adult talk."

Social life revolves around the front porch. Because the cottages are snug, the porch is the natural place to go for a little more elbow room. And because everyone walks in the neighborhood, it's easy to strike up a conversation. When Sally's husband tells her, "I'm going out to get the mail," she knows he might be out for an hour "or maybe more."

"When we came back every summer, it was like we never left our friends. We'd be in and out of each other's houses and roamed the neighborhood in packs."
—SALLY DAGNALL,
THE CAMPGROUND RESIDENT

Each pocket neighborhood at Oak Bluffs has its own character that changes with the generations. Wesleyan Circle, a cluster with about 10 cottages, currently has several young children and pets filling the circle with lively activity and sounds. Nearby Crystal Vincent Park is a quieter enclave with occasional visiting grandchildren. Some groups are quite sociable, with organized potlucks and apple pie socials; others enjoy "shared solitude."

## CAMPGROUND GOTHIC

A new American building type emerged with the campground cottages at Oak Bluff. Local carpenters combined Gothic and Romanesque styles using quickly fashioned wood, rather than stone and brick. This was a summer camp, not a cathedral at the end of a pilgrimage. Their flamboyant style reflected their religious experience. Using common materials and forms—45-degree gables, symmetrical facades, vertical siding, cantilevered balconies, window and door moldings, and ornamental trim—the carpenters created a unique style with infinite variation.

"The flamboyant style of the original cottages reflected the religious experience of the carpenters."

Facing page: The diminutive scale of the cottages has residents spilling out to the porch, where it's easy to engage in conversations with neighbors and passersby.

In the 1880s, porches began to be added. Their roofs, turned posts, and still more ornamentation changed the spatial character of the grounds by adding a middle space, open to view from passersby, yet functioning as semi-private outdoor rooms. Ever since, the porches have played a major role in hosting the social life of The Campground.

Today, that deeply social aspect remains at Oak Bluffs, even though the gatherings are fleeting, held during the warmer months. The dwellings here were built as summer cottages—with no insulation—and this is what gives them their prized character. Each year, when Labor Day passes, most residents go back to their winter homes. "Yet for so many of us," Sally Dagnall comments, "our summer friendships became lifelong friends, and we look forward to our next summer together."

23

## WHAT MAKES A GOOD PORCH?

The front porch is an essential facet of a pocket neighborhood. Its magic comes from the way it is both private and public, belonging to the household while being open to passersby. Making a good porch is both an art and a science.

**Get the Right Location.** This is the first step. A front porch is a place of transition, so make it part of the primary entrance, connected to the front yard and in full view of the street or public walkway.

**Make It a Living Space.** A porch gives a house its personal scale and animates the life of the street. Compare porches that seem to be merely surface décor—an effort to make a basic box more interesting—and porches that are clearly made for living in.

**Make It Large Enough.** Lingering hellos and goodbyes require a space about 5 ft. across. The minimum width is 6 ft. for an eating table and chairs, or a setting of porch rockers. I prefer 9 ft. to 10 ft. wide by about 12 ft. long. At this size the porch becomes a veritable room, an extension of the main living space.

**Don't Cut through the Middle.** Whatever you do, don't arrange a lane right through the middle of the gathering space. Place the passage to the front door to the side instead. If the porch is wide enough, the door may be centered between two gathering spaces.

**Keep the Porch Open.** It's tempting to enclose a porch. Remember though, that the porch contributes to the life of the public space, and making it too enclosed shifts the balance. Consider seasonal roll-down canvas curtains or fully removable storm windows to provide additional shelter when needed.

**Define the Edge.** A railing defines a critical social boundary between public and private realms. Don't leave it out. I like railings about 27 in. to 30 in. high—just the right balance of open and closed. It also happens to be just the right height for "perching" and for placing a cup of tea (provided it's wide enough). Make sure to check your building code: If the height from the deck to the ground is more than 30 in., most codes require the railing to be 36 in. or 42 in. high.

"Of porches there are two sorts: the decorative and the useful, the porch that is only a platform and the porch you can lie around on in your pajamas and read the Sunday paper."

—GARRISON KEILLOR (*WE ARE STILL MARRIED*, VIKING, 1989)

# CHAPTER 2
# Gardens of Compassion

Communities respond to the needs of the less fortunate in different ways.
Sometimes, those with the ability to help choose to ignore those living under
challenging conditions, whereas at other times misfortune can bring out the
best in their neighbors. Over the centuries, goodwill has occasionally taken
the form of pocket housing communities oriented around shared gardens.
A prime example is the *hofje* almshouses of the Netherlands.

# HOFJE ALMSHOUSES

In Europe, before there were retirement pensions, children typically looked after their parents in their old age. But what about people who didn't have children? They had to rely on the goodwill of extended family or the community. From the 15th through the 18th centuries in the Netherlands, at the time of the flourishing textile industry, some wealthy merchants founded almshouses to support people in need.

The Dutch word *hofje* refers to a form of privately funded socialized housing for the elderly with no children. *Hof* means "garden" and hofjes are small groups of apartment houses clustered around a courtyard or garden, similar in many ways to contemporary pocket neighborhoods. Most of the rent-free houses of the hofje were very simple living quarters consisting of a small room and sometimes a loft. These modest dwellings opened onto a community kitchen garden with a pump for rain or groundwater. Often they provided enough space for an orchard and a "bleaching-green" for sanitizing linens.

There were typically 8 to 10 apartment houses in a cluster, though some hofjes had as many as 25 units. These quiet refuges were not locked off from the outside world, but were accessed from the busy urban streets through a large door or gate. Their relative seclusion and small size offered residents an opportunity to look after one another while retaining their privacy.

Residents of a hofje lived under strict order, with expectations to be "pious, of good behavior, and clean." Before the Reformation, some were asked to pray for the founder. A porter distributed the daily beer, bread, and cheese, and peat in the winter to heat the houses.

There are dozens of hofjes still in existence in and around Amsterdam, Haarlem, Leiden, and other Dutch cities. Most are rented to students or low-wage working people or have become museums.

> "*Hof* means 'garden' and hofjes are small groups of apartments clustered around a courtyard or garden."

27

The quiet courtyards were typically located along a busy urban street and accessed through a large door or gate. Some hofjes were adjacent to small chapels.

# WORKINGMEN'S COTTAGES OF WARREN PLACE

Facing page: The central courtyard is a manicured formal garden, whereas the area in back (photo at bottom) is a relaxed and shifting mix of potted plants, personal projects, and café tables.

The cottages of Warren Place are a cluster of 30 row houses flanking a garden mews.

Responding to a similar impulse as the Dutch merchants, Alfred Tredway White, the son of a wealthy New York importer, built affordable housing for over a thousand working families in Brooklyn in the late 19th century. While making house calls to newly settled immigrants in his church district, White experienced firsthand the terrible living conditions of the urban poor. His efforts with housing reform created fireproof brick buildings with sunlit rooms and private toilets (what luxury!), always surrounding a shared green or park.

The Workingmen's Cottages of Warren Place, built in 1878, were a cluster of 30 row houses facing a garden mews and flanked by 4 end houses. Spanning between two parallel streets at mid-block, the formal garden is a semipublic space buffering the private entrances from the street. A second entrance is provided at the rear along a common, undivided walkway in the back. Each row house is just 11 ft. wide, 30 ft. deep, and three stories tall.

30

| Entry through a shared space.

## ALFRED TREDWAY WHITE'S PATTERNS
## FOR WARREN PLACE

Working well over 100 years ago, White understood the essential elements of making safe and healthy pocket neighborhoods. As you will see, these will appear as recurring themes throughout this book.

**Human Scale.** Warren Place is a neighborhood within a neighborhood. A sensible number of households—in this case 30—share a common garden, which brings residents into daily contact with one another and strengthens the bonds of caring.

**A Garden at the Center.** White felt that everyone—even the poorest of the poor—should have direct and daily contact with nature. Looking out to green leaves and birds softens the urban experience.

**Narrow Buildings.** When every building is only two rooms deep, there is ample sunlight and cross-ventilation in every space.

**Entry through a Shared Space.** Residents walking home through the central mews or informal back garden are likely to pass neighbors and stop for a chat. These spontaneous meetings help to build community.

**Eyes on the Commons.** If active rooms of a house look onto the shared commons, residents can see who is a guest and who is a stranger. The commons is "claimed" as a territory belonging to all the neighbors, and as a result will be safer and well used.

**Connection and Contribution.** Shared spaces have life when bordering buildings and gardens all work together. The end houses at Warren Place add to the interest of the street with their overlooking windows and flower boxes; the central row houses are adorned with richly patterned red brick; the backs of the houses have been personalized by the residents. Every aspect connects and contributes to creating a special quality. Nothing is forgotten; nothing is left over.

**Snug Quarters.** Given the intimacy of the living spaces, residents often extend out into public space—socializing on the front stoop,

A garden at the center.

setting up a coffee table along the back walk, or claiming space for a flower bed. This is a good thing. In standard suburban developments, people typically have all their needs met within their own home and seldom interact with their neighbors.

**Ownership and Stewardship.** Rather than hiring an outside management company to maintain the commons and handle the budget, residents serve on a board to do it themselves. They naturally step forward to guide additional improvement projects and organize activities such as tag sales, holiday parties, and garden volunteer days.

## CHAPTER 3

# Visions of Garden Cities

Many contemporary pocket neighborhoods stem from the vision of English social idealist Ebenezer Howard. In 1898, Howard wrote a book entitled *Garden Cities of Tomorrow,* in which he offered a vision of cities free of the ill effects of industrialization. He called for the creation of new towns of limited size, supported by their local industry and surrounded by a permanent "green belt" of agricultural land.

Howard was not a designer. Yet in 1903, his detailed descriptions and diagrams attracted enough attention and backing to begin developing Letchworth Garden City near London to test the ideas. The success of this model new town sparked the imagination of planners and developers across Europe, Australia, and America, and eventually influenced future thinking about zoning laws and town planning. The New Urbanism movement, which began in the United States in the early 1980s, incorporates many of Howard's concepts. And Walt Disney used elements of Howard's vision in his design for the Experimental Prototype Community of Tomorrow (EPCOT). Although Howard did not call for "pocket neighborhoods" per se, the projects that emerged from his utopian thinking were human scaled and based on social relationships of nearby neighbors.

Located 20 minutes from midtown Manhattan by subway, Forest Hills Gardens surprises first-time visitors with its contrasts. Stepping from the bustling commercial district into the brick-paved public square, it feels like being in a nineteenth-century European town.

# FOREST HILLS GARDENS

Ebenezer Howard's ideas first surfaced in America in 1909 with the planning of Forest Hills Gardens in the Borough of Queens in New

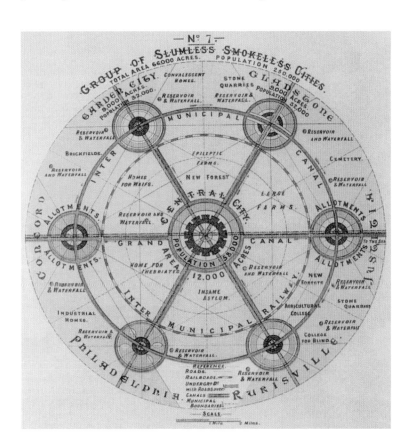

Ebenezer Howard had a grand vision for cities free of the ill effects of industrialization. He called for communities surrounded by green belts, with balanced areas of residences, industry, and agriculture.

York City. Renowned landscape architect Frederick Law Olmsted Jr. and architect Grosvenor Atterbury led the charge to design a verdant pedestrian-scale village of 900 homes, townhouses, and apartment buildings, with a commercial hub and public school. Included are house clusters and short, defined blocks with shared common greens. More than 100 years later, their plan remains intact, a testament to their vision.

Olmsted and Atterbury were masterful choreographers of social space. They laid out an array of gently curving streets, small parks, pedestrian walkways, and a variety of housing types and forms—all with an eye toward quiet comfort. Olmsted introduced innovative methods to calm traffic (for what that meant in 1909): T-intersections, sequences of one-way streets, and roadway widths corresponding to the amount of traffic they intended. Short blocks became pocket neighborhoods, with brick entry portals at the ends of each block and a landscaped "close" at the center. Clusters of buildings were organized to define shared gardens. At the center of Forest Hills Gardens is an elementary school and a community building for cultural and recreational activities.

Above: Short blocks between parallel streets have brick entry portals at the ends and a landscaped "close" at the center.

Facing page: Multiple-unit buildings laid out around a shared garden fit seamlessly with single-family homes in the neighborhood.

## The Legacy of Forest Hills Gardens

The legacy of this neighborhood is a mixed one, reflecting both the possibilities and the limitations of planning and design. Olmsted, Atterbury, and their colleagues created an inspiring model of an enduring, human-scaled community. The original goal of this project was to provide residents of moderate income a healthy alternative to urban living. It was never meant as a private, gated enclave or an exclusive address for the wealthy. Yet in the decades following its construction, the Gardens' generous layout and exquisite detail stood well above all else, and home prices rose beyond what the middle class could afford.

36

## SUNNYSIDE GARDENS

About 10 years after Forest Hills Gardens was completed, a group of
planners and architects, including Lewis Mumford, Clarence Stein, and
Henry Wright, were inspired by Ebenezer Howard's vision. They traveled
to England to see the new garden cities firsthand, and returned with a
passion to build a garden city in America.

Their initial plan was ambitious: a complete new city of 25,000
people—looking very much like New Urbanist towns of today—on the
outskirts of New York City. However, the challenge of securing and
financing 640 contiguous acres was insurmountable, and the grand
scheme was never realized. So they set their sights on 56 acres in an
undeveloped area of Queens near a train station and persuaded an
amenable developer to join them in building Sunnyside Gardens.

The first group of buildings, constructed in 1924, was designed as a subcommunity within the larger neighborhood. In other words, it was a pocket neighborhood. Connected one- and two-family houses surrounded the perimeter of the block, each with a narrow garden at the street and a larger private backyard. The largest portion at the center of the block was held for common use as a shared garden and playground, under the control of a homeowner's association.

As Sunnyside was developed, more blocks were built with central common areas, but the form and use evolved. Noise from children was annoying to some, so a dedicated playground was established at the edge of the neighborhood, and the common greens were reserved for visual respite and quiet gatherings. The 900-ft.-long blocks were subdivided into three or four clusters of about 36 houses, with each commons opening to the next. This seemed like an appropriate social unit.

Stein and Wright focused on providing maximum livability at minimum cost. Building-plan types were limited and their layouts were efficient and simple (in other words, snug). Details were standardized and plain. At the same time, aesthetic concerns were not overlooked. By varying building heights and setbacks, they created a pleasing architectural rhythm that shaped the outdoor spaces. Taller three-family homes anchored the corners of the clusters to give the central garden just the right degree of enclosure. Cluster layouts shifted slightly from one block to the next so that views from the crosswalks terminated on a gabled face of a building across the street.

Long blocks are divided into clusters of townhouses and stacked apartments, with shared gardens at the center. Narrow walkways connect one courtyard to another and to the street.

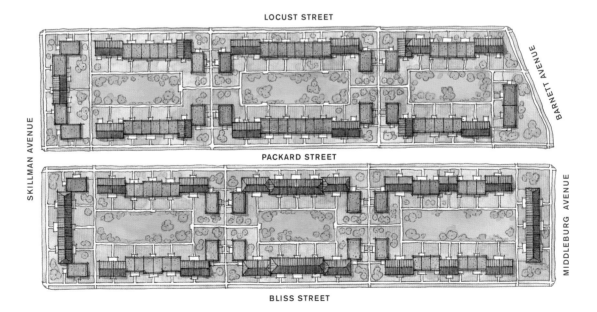

Some groups of apartments open directly to landscaped common areas running perpendicular to the street, while others have entries off of narrow, tree-lined streets, with back doors that open to private yards and a central commons at the interior of the block.

"Like Olmsted, Stein and Wright dared put beauty as one of the imperative needs of a planned environment: the beauty of ordered buildings, measured to the human scale, of trees and flowering plants, and of open greens surrounded by buildings of low density."
—LEWIS MUMFORD, CITY PLANNING HISTORIAN AND RESIDENT OF SUNNYSIDE GARDENS

Above: Networks of alleyways weave through the commons areas and to the streets. Many of the crosswalks line up with the gabled ends of taller buildings, the result of a careful shift of cluster pattern from one block to the next.

Left: Today, although the architecture of Sunnyside Gardens remains largely intact, many of the commons areas have grown into a tangle of untended shrubs and trees. They have become wild parks that offer relief from urban life, yet buffer individual households from one another—a new reality that seems contrary to the original intent of the commons drawing neighbors together.

# RADBURN

Radburn was envisioned as an ambitious plan for the "motor age," a model community that was safe for children, yet linked to the city.

Early in 1928, after the successful "dress rehearsal" at Sunnyside, Stein, Wright, and their development team were ready to carry out their original objective to build a complete garden city. Economic trends pointed skyward and they set off with an ambitious plan, one that addressed the changing reality of development in the United States.

During the 30 years after the appearance of Howard's *Garden Cities of Tomorrow*, the automobile had become a dominant factor in planning. There were 21 million cars registered in America at that time, so they determined that Radburn must be "A Plan for the Motor Age, where people could live peacefully with the automobile—or rather in spite of it" (*Toward New Towns for America*, MIT Press, 1966).

The Radburn team secured two square miles of land on the New Jersey side of the newly opened George Washington Bridge linking to Manhattan. Their plan was to develop a series of three connected residential neighborhoods for an eventual population of 25,000.

TOWN PLAN
RADBURN, N.J.

The town plan for Radburn was designed in 1928 for 25,000 people in three connected neighborhoods. A necklace of parks allowed residents to walk to shops and school without encountering cars. One third of the plan was completed before the Great Depression put a stop to development, yet it was enough to demonstrate the validity of the idea.

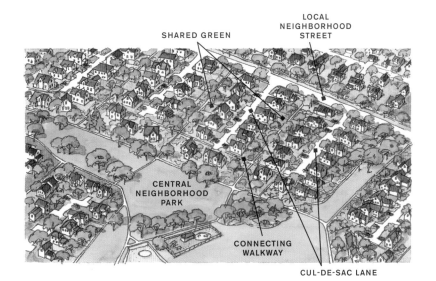

Pocket neighborhood clusters of about 14 houses each have access from cul-de-sac lanes and "front" onto a shared green with the next cluster. These tie into the central neighborhood commons and elementary school.

Above top: A network of walkways connects the neighborhoods and parks—all separated from roadways.

Above bottom: At the center of the neighborhood is an elementary school.

## THE RADBURN PLAN

The Radburn Plan included multiple levels of scale, from paths and gardens, to houses, pocket neighborhood clusters, and "superblocks," all within neighborhoods in a ten-minute walking radius.

**"Superblock."** This was a term for the basic neighborhood "unit" of about 35 to 50 acres, bounded by collector streets, and with a landscaped park at its core. Each superblock contains about a dozen smaller pocket neighborhoods within it.

**Hierarchy of Roads.** Roadways are differentiated into service lanes that provide direct access to buildings, collector streets at the perimeter of the superblocks, through-roads linking neighborhoods and districts, and express highways and parkways for connection to outside communities.

**Separation of Pedestrians and Cars.** Walkways and paths tie directly into a system of connected parks and nearby neighborhoods through under- or overpasses—all without crossing a roadway.

**Cul-de-sacs.** These were the precursors to the suburban cul-de-sacs built across America, with this critical difference: Radburn cul-de-sacs have walkways connecting with other house clusters and the central green, so residents are not "locked in." Also, Radburn streets are narrower.

**Pocket Neighborhoods.** A limited number of houses—about a dozen per access lane—form a cluster. The "fronts" of the homes face onto a shared green with the next cluster.

**A School at the Center.** An elementary school is located at the hub of the community.

**Shops and Businesses at the Entrance.** To provide a stronger economic base for businesses, the main commercial center was located at the entrance to Radburn to serve a wider area than Radburn's center alone.

# THE LEGACY OF
# THE GARDEN CITY VISION

Compelling ideas have a lineage that can be traced through time. Threads of Howard's vision of garden cities carried on beyond Radburn to appear in new towns, such as Greenbelt, Maryland (1935), Reston, Virginia (1964), and Seaside, Florida (1979). The town of Vallingby, Sweden, outside of Stockholm, was built after World War II and was one of the best early examples of a comprehensive vision, as are Canberra, Australia, and Brasilia, Brasil. Village Homes in Davis, California, built in the 1970s, introduced the dimension of solar orientation and energy use to the vision (see pp. 124–133).

Although good ideas often evolve into something even better, they can also morph into pale imitations or even the opposite of the original intent. As Frank Lloyd Wright's Prairie style home became the ubiquitous and mediocre Ranch style tract house, Radburn's intimate and connected cul-de-sacs became dead-end lollipop cul-de-sacs of suburban America, and clearly defined superblocks became the basis for amorphous sprawl.

Above top: Pedestrian paths extend from the end of the cul-de-sacs.

Above bottom: Radburn was a revolutionary plan with bad timing. Months after the first homeowners moved in, the stock market collapsed. The grand idea never saw the light of day, yet enough of the plan was constructed to demonstrate a new town form and inspire planners and builders throughout the world.

## CHAPTER 4

# Bungalow Courts, Walks, and Walk Streets

At the same time the garden cities idea was being explored on the East Coast in the early 1900s, a new type of housing was evolving in southern California that made the dream of a house and a garden attainable for the working class. This was the bungalow court.

The format was quite simple: a series of small, individual cottages arranged in parallel rows, with their living rooms and porches facing a shared garden (a pattern common to many contemporary pocket neighborhoods). Cars were parked to the side, or off of an alley behind the court.

This basic pattern, with a number of variations, was repeated on infill lots in city after city throughout the region. Small developers were attracted to the layout because the courts were highly profitable as rental properties. Bungalow courts could easily be adapted to a larger residential lot, or a cluster of two to four lots, at a much higher density than the surrounding single-family homes. Newly relocated residents and long-stay tourists found an affordable alternative to apartments and hotels, and a kind of instant community that offered stability and order in their new world. These courts blended the benefits of a single-family home (privacy, gardens, and porches) with the convenience of an apartment (low rent and minimal maintenance).

Even though the configuration introduced housing at a density of four to six times that of surrounding homes, the courts fit seamlessly into the neighborhood. The two houses at the front of the court typically offered a pleasing facade to the street that related well to the adjacent single-family houses. Passersby had an intriguing glimpse into the central garden, and parked cars were virtually unseen.

The result created a broader variety of housing options within the wider community, which attracted a healthy diversity of ages, income levels, and household sizes.

Above and facing page: Bowen Court (1910–1912) is the oldest court in Pasadena and one of the largest courts in southern California. It has 25 Craftsman bungalows arranged around a central garden courtyard. Bungalow courtyards proliferated throughout southern California during the early 1900s, offering affordable housing and a sense of community in a garden setting.

45

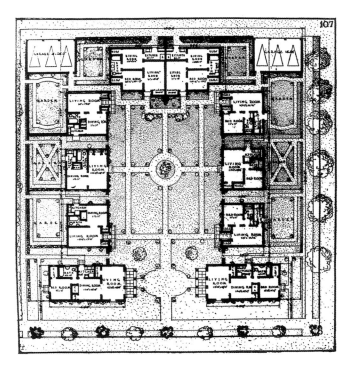

Early bungalow courts featured two homes at the head of the court that related equally well to the street and the courtyard. Behind them were as many pairs of homes as would fit the depth of the lot, with a central pair anchoring the rear. Cars were parked to the side or off of an alley.

# ORIGINS AND EVOLUTION

The idea for the bungalow court may have derived from East Coast resort communities such as Oak Bluffs (see pp. 20–23), where tents and cabins were organized around a central commons, or it may have been a natural merging of the popular Craftsman bungalow home with the historic Spanish Mission courtyards of the region. Whatever its origin, the first bungalow court appeared in 1909, St. Francis Court, reportedly the invention of architect Sylvanus Marston for a developer in Pasadena, California. It was an upscale design intended for well-to-do tourists, complete with Tiffany lamps and Stickley furniture. Most of the courts that followed, however, were predominantly downscale, designed by contractors for working-class people with fewer choices. The contractors built for profit, and most likely had little understanding of the courts' social or historic value.

> "Few urban housing forms have proven so successful in serving—simultaneously— density, privacy, and community as the bungalow court."
> —KEVIN STARR, HISTORIAN

Proponents of the Arts & Crafts ideal spoke out against bungalow courts. Charles Sumner Greene, who designed the epitome of California Craftsman style—the Gamble House—wrote in *The Architect* magazine in 1915, "The bungalow court idea is to be regretted. Born of the ever-persistent speculator, ... it would seem to have no other reason for being than that of making money for the investor. The style and design of each unit is uniform, making for the monotony and dreariness of a factory district. This is an example of what not to do."

Bungalow courts, however, met real needs of a burgeoning population, and flourished throughout California. In Pasadena alone, there were 414 bungalow courts by 1933, accommodating 8 percent of its 81,000 residents.

The success of the form comes, in part, from the ease with which it could adapt to lot dimensions and the wide variety of styles that were possible. The early courts, dating from 1910 to 1916, were mostly built in a "U" pattern on lots with a frontage of 150 ft. or more and a depth as great. This allowed for a central garden space 50 ft. wide, with room for porches, small private yards, and significant landscaping in the shared court. As land prices increased after World War I, the courts were built on diminishingly narrower lots, to about 75 ft. wide, with the common space taking up the slack. A half-court pattern appeared on an even narrower lot, in an "L"-shaped configuration. Pushing the limits further, some court layouts morphed into a series of one- or two-sided attached garden apartments.

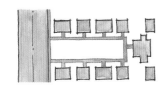

DETACHED WIDE COURT (ENCLOSED)

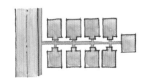

DETACHED NARROW COURT (ENCLOSED)

HALF COURT OR L-SHAPED

California Craftsman style dominated the early bungalow courts. In later years, revival styles appeared, including Mission, Spanish Colonial, American Colonial, English Cottage, and Tudor. Art Deco worked just as successfully. This style, that style, it didn't matter—as long as each building fit within the collective of the whole group.

48

## EXOTIC APARTMENT COURTS

Courtyard housing took hold in Los Angeles in part because of similarities between California and Mediterranean climates, as well as the local heritage of Spanish missions. As Hollywood's new movie industry was creating period epics, imaginative minds were tapping into rich image libraries of these film studios to inspire exotic, Mediterranean-style garden apartment courts.

Although most bungalow courts featured very modest dwellings designed and built by contractors, architects became increasingly involved in designing exotic apartment courts for the upper middle class, most notably near Hollywood. Fertile imaginations were influenced by movie set designs and the extensive libraries of the studios that documented Mediterranean courtyard details, especially those of Southern Spain.

Courts such as the Andalusia and El Cabrillo are garden oases with tiled fountains, outdoor fireplaces, and lush plantings. Some of their more famous residents included movie stars Greta Garbo, Clara Bow, and Cesar Romero.

# THE ENDURING LEGACY OF BUNGALOW COURTS

The Great Depression brought a halt to most development, and by the time the economy kicked in after World War II, the American Dream had changed its tune and the bungalow court was all but forgotten. Forgotten for a time. Architects and planners are now revisiting the bungalow courts and drawing lessons that can apply to present-day needs.

"Bungalow courts get it right," says Rick Cole, former mayor of Pasadena and proponent of New Urbanism. "They're elegant, simple, and easily readable. You know where the boundaries are between the public street and the semi-public courtyard, the semi-private porch and the private interior living space. It's all coherently organized."

This coherence makes the common space more secure. When someone walks into a bungalow court, neighbors can recognize who is a stranger and who belongs. And on a social level, the courtyard is where neighbors nod and say hello, and begin to forge ties that grow into friendships and connections of mutual benefit. Impromptu suppers, babysitting arrangements, word about a possible job opportunity—these are the threads that weave a community together. The bungalow court makes this easy. Perhaps that is its most enduring legacy.

## MO-TEL: TAKING THE SHOW ON THE ROAD

The bungalow court can trace its roots to the garden oases of Southern Spain and Morocco, yet it contained the seeds of the motel in America. Arthur Heineman, who designed Bowen Court, registered the word "mo-tel" in 1925 with his first design for an auto court, and the idea caught on across the country. In an ironic switch, the central garden courtyard was given over to the automobile, replacing the epitome of a sense of place and community with an expression of mobility and alienation.

CAPITOL AUTO COURT
BOISE, IDAHO
*"One of the Most Modern Courts in the West"*

# WALKS AND WALK STREETS

Whereas bungalow courts are enclosed courtyards, "walks" are garden passageways flanked by homes on either side leading from one street to the next at midblock. They are a kind of pocket neighborhood that welcomes surrounding neighbors.

## Maybeck's Rose Walk

The namesake of this type of walk is a celebrated garden path named Rose Walk, designed in 1913 by Bernard Maybeck in the Berkeley Hills to link residents in an upper neighborhood to a streetcar line below. Maybeck did not design the houses, beyond skillfully placing their position; yet the houses, walkway, trees, and views seem woven as a whole.

Stepping off the busy street and up the curved staircase to a quiet, landscaped walk is an emotional experience. A choreography of space unfolds, with intimate garden views, cedar-clad Craftsman homes, resting spots, and long vistas. It was a simple, brilliant gesture that expressed Maybeck's vision. Known for his mystical persuasion, he said, "Sooner

Bernard Maybeck's Rose Walk in the Berkeley Hills is a beloved walk and cascade of steps that links an uphill neighborhood with a transit line.

or later cities will express the highest spiritual life that they are capable of." Or, in the words of one uphill resident, "On a clear morning, there's nothing better."

The street in front of these homes has been a pedestrian space since the streets were platted nearly 100 years ago. Automobile and service access is via alleys at the rear of the homes.

## Walk Streets of Manhattan Beach

Several blocks off the ocean shore at Manhattan Beach in southern California you'll find a series of walk streets constructed between 1913 and 1928. This pattern has narrow lots that front on paved pedestrian lanes, about 15 ft. wide, which tie into connector streets at each end. Garages and service vehicles access the homes from alleyways running parallel to these walk streets.

On a summer evening, children of all ages are playing in these lanes, with not a car in sight. Two girls take turns shooting a basketball at a hoop set up in the middle. Another youngster is playing with plastic bowling pins on a chalked pattern drawn on the concrete. A mother walks up with a cartful of groceries, chatting to neighbors having dinner in their yard. These are all signs of being in a healthy pocket neighborhood.

## CHARACTERISTICS OF WALK STREETS

Not surprisingly, walk streets and pocket neighborhoods have a lot in common:

- Cars are held at bay.
- Children have a play zone beyond their own yard.
- Parents' concern for their children's safety is eased, because parents know that other adults are looking on or listening.

- The shared common area is a clearly felt "territory" where strangers are noted.
- Layers of openness and privacy provide easily read messages for neighbors: "I'm open for a chat" or "Do not disturb."

## CHAPTER 5

# Cottage Court Revival

Seattle developer John Kucher saw promise in the tiny tumbledown cottages. He was referring to the ten small—as in 400-sq.-ft. small—rental houses sitting vacant in a part of town where drug deals were the neighborhood corner conversation. Other developers would have torn the shells down and built a no-frills apartment building. Kucher restored the cottages, helped turn the neighborhood around, and built a bellwether for a pocket neighborhood revival.

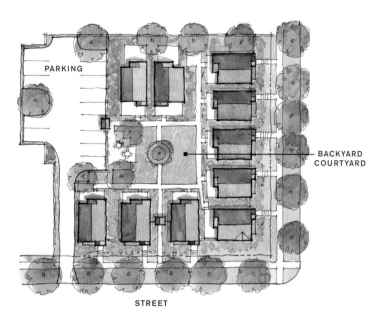

STREET

The Pine Street Cottages had been left abandoned and would have been demolished had a far-sighted developer not seen their potential.

53

The cottages were originally built in 1916 as affordable rentals for Seattle's growing workforce. "My dad started with one house. Then kept building one at a time around in a circle," says Jim Hammock, who recently turned 100 years old and worked as a "go-fer" on the construction crew. They weren't aware of the bungalow courts being built about the same time (see pp. 44–49), but the effect was very similar. The backs of the houses faced onto a shared courtyard tended by all, which cultivated an informal community among the backyard neighbors.

Ten small cottages surround a shared backyard court with porches looking on. Residents can enter through the front door off of the street, or park their cars in a side lot and enter the back door through the courtyard.

## WORKING WITH THE NEIGHBORS

Before beginning renovation in 1990, Kucher was approached by the producer of *America's Most Wanted* and two undercover narcotics officers, who wanted to use the site for a reenactment of a drive-by shooting. True story. On reflection, it didn't seem like such a bad idea to Kucher: If they would help get rid of the three crack houses on the street, they had their site. It was a deal.

Kucher's initial idea was to build a fortress-like fence on the street to provide security for the residents. Vandalism was out of control. He engaged the next-door neighbor, a retired military man who had trained security guards, to help look after the construction site. Turns out a pack of young kids were throwing rocks through the windows at night. "We turned them into our 'rock police' with a bargain," says Kucher. "If any windows were broken, they didn't get any money. But every week that went by with no windows broken, they got paid." It worked.

Mail is delivered to a common drop-off just inside the covered gateway.

As time went on, Kucher got to know more neighbors and started to rethink the fence idea. With the crack dealers gone, it seemed the front yards could be given back to the neighborhood. Architect Marcia Gamble-Hadley, who worked with Kucher on the project, suggested moving the fences back so they would line up with the front of the cottages and open the front yards to the street.

Gamble-Hadley describes these kinds of gestures as making a streetscape "participatory." At the front gate she designed a little dog-watering dish, with a foot pedal that fills the dish to the rim. "On a hot walk, dogs need water," she explains with matter-of-fact empathy.

"What is interesting about our project," says Kucher, "was the way it evolved. As we'd be there working and talking with neighbors and the crew, we'd learn things, and then make changes in response." No doubt this was part of their recipe for its magical quality.

## NEW MARKETS

Before small houses became a big thing, the idea of renovating a 410-sq.-ft. house on speculation seemed like a bad idea. Who could even shoehorn themselves into a tiny box? Well, ten buyers snapped them up quickly for about $85,000. They were urban singles and couples, predominantly 30- and 40-something professionals. The developers tapped an unrecognized niche market, but not the condo crowd. These buyers had no tolerance for hearing a neighbor's toilet flush, or a constant churning of personalities and vehicles. They wanted to live in a ground-based single-family neighborhood, without the long to-do lists that come with family-size houses.

"When you build a small cottage," says Gamble-Hadley, "your clientele self selects." Anybody who thinks "bigger is better" is not even going to shop for a house smaller than a bedroom suite in a McMansion. She observes that people who will buy a cottage are the ones who find simplicity appealing. "They love living small, where everything is within easy reach and quick to clean, where they can

The front entry porches (left and facing page, bottom) are an important facet of the neighborhood texture and are designed carefully for both function and security. At the time of their renovation it was a rough neighborhood, so they couldn't be so deep as to create blind spots. The porches needed to provide just enough shelter from the rain and serve as convenience perches to place bags while negotiating keys.

be masters of all their inner dust bunnies." She believes a small space is not a detriment for this market, but rather an attraction. A willingness to accept small space is not enough, however. It has to perform. As in a boat, everything has to be well fitted with a place and purpose.

## LIVING LARGE IN A SMALL HOUSE

With so little space, every niche and nook is utilized. The original bathroom opened awkwardly into the main room. The access was redirected, and the 4-in. cavity of the doorway was filled in with 16 lineal feet of shelves, only one or two commodities deep—perfect for a bottle

Small spaces can live large:
The original low ceilings were
opened up to create a vaulted
space with skylights (right), and
a doorway cavity was retrofitted
as a bathroom storage solution
(below).

of contact lens solution, makeup, and medicines. There is even an electrical outlet for a clock radio and electric toothbrush.

But even nifty storage solutions and outlets in the right spots don't sell a house. A small house must also have delight and charm to attract this kind of buyer. At the Pine Street Cottages, delight begins with the basic volume and shape of a space, and the way the space is filled with natural light. The original low, claustrophobic ceilings were taken out to create a vaulted space with exposed tie-rafters, painted all white to give a more spacious feel. A skylight floods the interior with light, brightening even the grayest of Seattle days.

Kucher set out to counter the prevailing notion that small means cheap. A solid brass handle greets you at the front door—not a knock-off copy, but the real thing—setting an indelible impression of character and quality. "If we took the low-grade route," Kucher commented, "we would have missed this market and run the risk of alienating the neighbors." He took the effort to restore the classic Craftsman detail on the exteriors. Inside, this quality continues: hardwood flooring, solid wood doors trimmed with period molding, handcrafted painted finishes, and built-in cupboards. These houses have what Vitruvius wrote about over 2,000 years ago: "firmness, comfort, and delight." It worked in his time, and it works in ours.

> "Rather than a fad, cottage courtyards are a bellwether, because living more densely is not only a responsible thing to do environmentally and economically, but it also creates more of a sense of togetherness and social responsibility."
> —MARCIA GAMBLE-HADLEY, ARCHITECT

## A NEW COTTAGE CODE

The Pine Street Cottages were an immediate hit, which prompted interest in building new versions. But it was not an easy road. City zoning laws prohibited development with this much density, so Kucher and others helped the city write a new cottage courtyard housing ordinance. They soon found out that both cottages and density were hot buttons. A few vocal residents were vehemently opposed to introducing tiny houses into their neighborhoods of larger, single-family homes out of fear of more traffic, noise, and degradation of their property values. In the end, the city backed off and adopted the ordinance for multifamily zones only, where high land values make cottage courtyard housing unrealistic. The work on the code, however, was not all in vain, as we shall see in Chapter 6.

# PART TWO

# CONTEMPORARY POCKET NEIGHBORHOODS

**Patterns of community are perennial.** We respond emotionally to timeless historic patterns of pocket neighborhoods: the almshouse apartments opening onto *hofje* gardens; the cluster of gingerbread cottages with porches overlooking a shared commons; the mother pulling her son in a wagon through a community green; the quiet enclave behind a group of workman's cottages.

> "The fundamental unit of organization within the neighborhood is the cluster of a dozen houses."
> —CHRISTOPHER ALEXANDER

Fast forward to the present day, and we still look for signs of these timeless patterns. Here and there, the fundamental forms emerge again in clarity, and we feel their integrity. Mostly though, other form-giving forces give shape to our built environment that are less responsive to basic human and social needs: zoning laws that make walking difficult, if not impossible; road construction requirements engineered more for traffic speed than pedestrian safety; development budgets and processes focused on profit rather than community building.

Planning, engineering, and development need not be at odds with the fundamental patterns of community. The pocket neighborhoods in this section show developments that celebrate the beauty of neighbors gathered around a shared commons. These communities balance the layers of personal and social space, introduce cars into a neighborhood without dominating pedestrian space, and even show streets as the shared "rooms" of a pocket neighborhood.

To rephrase Christopher Alexander, the basic building block of community is the cluster of a few houses gathered together to foster neighborly relationships. These contemporary pocket neighborhoods show that housing development is more than building houses; they show patterns of development that build community.

# CHAPTER 6
# A New Cottage Court

Sometimes, innovation takes root in unlikely places. A good example of this happened in the small town of Langley, where I live with about a thousand other people on the outskirts of Seattle. In 1995, following Seattle's failed attempt at passing an ordinance that would allow new projects like Pine Street Cottages (see Chapter 5), Jack Lynch, our city planner, introduced the concept to his planning board. It seemed to fit the bill for preserving housing diversity, affordability, and neighborhood character, and was readily approved—making it the first ordinance of its kind in the country to become law.

Langley's new cottage courtyard housing code was focused on expanding the choices for households of one and two people. Even though this segment represents more than 60 percent of households in America, the building industry pushes family-size houses almost exclusively. The new ordinance counters this tendency with an incentive that allows twice the number of homes than normally allowed in residential zones. The catch is that house size is limited to 700 sq. ft. on the ground level and no more than 975 sq. ft. total, including a second floor. Such an increase in density comes from the recognition that cottage-size homes have less impact than their plus-size cousins.

In addition to the size limitation, the code stipulates that the cottages must face a usable landscaped common area, have a livable-size porch, and have parking screened from the street. To ensure a good fit within existing neighborhoods, each proposed project must be reviewed by both the planning and design review boards.

Third Street Cottages marked a contemporary resurgence of pocket neighborhoods and set the stage for others that followed.

Eight cottages and Commons Buildings fit onto a ⅔-acre site with parking tucked in along the side. It was a model that demonstrated a strong market for small homes in a community setting.

## TESTING THE CODE

When this new code was passed in my own town, I didn't have any intention of becoming a developer to test its viability. I was focused on designing individual "sensibly sized" homes, tailored to fit homeowners' needs without a lot of unnecessary space. It was my response to the waves of oversize, garage-fronted houses I saw everywhere I traveled in America. In the face of "bigger is better," my mantra was "small is beautiful."

Jim Soules made the link between my custom cottages and the new code. We met at a presentation I made to a builder's group about designing smaller houses. His background was very different from mine—he had been a planner, tract-housing builder, and affordable housing developer, as well as a Peace Corps volunteer. But we were equally exasperated by the mediocrity of large-scale development. He was inspired by the vitality he felt in my small houses, and knowing about the new cottage courtyard code, suggested we build a cluster of cottages in Langley. We gathered our savings, rallied our relatives into joining us, purchased four adjoining lots in town, and then set out to test the strength of an unknown market.

63

At the entrance from the public street, residents pick up their mail, perhaps linger in a conversation with a neighbor, and pass through an "implied gate" along a narrowed walkway leading to the semi-public courtyard beyond.

## DISCOVERING THE KEY DESIGN PRINCIPLES

Planning requirements are based on intentions and goals, but a plan in real life must address the specifics of a site, as well as personal and social needs. For example, how do neighbors live close together while preserving privacy between them? How does a courtyard community, with an inward focus, relate to the surrounding neighborhood? How can a single person feel safe while living alone?

We had an idea of the right direction to take, but we found inspiration while visiting the Pine Street Cottages. We were moved by the intimate scale of its buildings and gardens, and by its shared courtyard space. It felt like a quiet refuge apart from the bustle of the city. Sitting out front on the curb, we sketched out a plan for Third Street Cottages in about 15 minutes.

## DESIGNING FOR COMMUNITY

The plan for Third Street Cottages broadly followed the layout of the Pine Street Cottages (see pp. 52–57), but introduced several new design principles to make it work for today's homeowner. We used the following principles:

**Connection and Contribution.** Any site belongs within a larger context while also shaping and giving detail to this context. So the first question in design is asking how a plan can connect and contribute to its surroundings.

**Cottage Scale.** If twice the density of dwellings is allowed in a single-family zone, the houses need to be smaller in scale to lessen the impact on the surrounding neighborhood. Therefore, Third Street Cottages are 1½-story cottages, not 2-story houses.

**Individuality.** Though similar to the others, each cottage is unique. This individuality fosters a personal bond of caring and identity between each homeowner and his or her home. We carefully chose exterior colors for each cottage in relation to one another—a total of 24 different colors—which clearly differentiates one cottage from another. Each household creates its own garden landscape and flowerbox garden. Some are like overgrown English cottage gardens, whereas others are simple and Zenlike. But they all complement each other.

**Corralling the Car.** Cars dominate our lives to a great degree, so it's critical that they are kept in check. We intentionally placed parking away from the cottages and screened it from the street, which lets residents walk through the commons to their front doors. This arrangement creates an opportunity to smell the flowers or talk with a neighbor in the flow of daily life. Although considered controversial by some, it has not proven to be a hardship.

The street face of the community extends a friendly gesture, even while the cottages face inward toward the courtyard.

Parking is tucked in pockets away from the street.

**Layering from Public to Private.** A sequence of boundaries defines increasingly private layers of personal space. A resident arriving home or a guest coming to visit enters through "implied" gateways—near the mailbox kiosk or the parking pockets—into the garden courtyard. From here to the front door there are five more layers: a border of perennial plantings, a low split-cedar fence with a swinging gate, the front yard, the frame of the porch with a porch railing and flowerboxes, and the porch itself. Within the cottages, the layering continues, with active spaces toward the commons and private spaces further back and above.

The layering of personal space continues inside, with the most private rooms located to the back and in lofts above.

**Eyes on the Commons.** The first line of defense for personal security is a strong network of neighbors who know and care for one another. When kitchens and dining areas look onto the shared common areas, a stranger is noticed and neighbors can easily be called on in an emergency.

**Nested Houses.** To ensure privacy between cottages, the houses "nest" together: the "open" side of one house faces the "closed" side of the next. You could say the houses are spooning. The open side has large windows facing its side yard (which extends to the face of the neighboring house), whereas the closed side has high windows and skylights. This arrangement ensures that neighbors do not look into one another's worlds, allowing a measure of privacy.

Facing page: Active indoor rooms look out to the shared commons.

66

This page: Careful placement of windows ensures privacy for nested houses.

All cottages face a garden at the center.

The Commons Building has a ground-floor workshop/gathering space and a roof-top terrace.

**A Commons at the Heart.** With all paths leading through and all cottages facing the commons, this is the center of the community. A pea-patch garden lies at one end, a calm stretch of lawn at the other. A child's swing hangs from the heirloom plum tree at the center. To the side is the workshop—the place to cane a chair, start spring seedlings, and gather for parties. On the roof is a terrace with a terrific overview. A tool shed provides a spot for shared garden implements.

**Porch Rooms.** So many porches these days are faux add-ons, cartoonish appliqués that may look like porches but have absolutely no function except to offer "curb appeal." A porch should be large enough to be a room and placed just off of the active area of the house. It should also be next to the commons, where householders can choose to engage informally with neighbors. The passageway to the front door should pass along the side and not the center of the porch, to preserve its function as a room.

Left: Inexpensive materials, detailed well, can create delightful spaces.

Below: The main living areas are all on the first-floor level for accessibility. Lofts are used as TV rooms, writing and creative project studios, and kids' play areas.

**Living Large in a Small House.** A small house can feel and function large when there is ample light and adequate storage space. Ceilings 9 ft. and higher with large windows and skylights fill the rooms with light, creating a much larger perceived sense of space. Ample storage is provided, with walk-in closets, an attic, and an exterior storage room. Built-in shelves, alcoves, and nooks take less space than furniture and offer charm. All the main living areas are on the first floor, and there is a spacious full-height loft accessed by a ship's ladder.

**Simple Materials, Rich Detail.** Standard, off-the-shelf materials create a rich layering of texture. The details are honest but not fussy, a delight to the eye: We used reclaimed, whitewashed spruce paneling, brightly painted Dutch doors, vinyl windows with traditional white painted trim, plywood and batten ceilings, stained Medite® flooring, and no drywall.

# FROM VISION TO REALITY

Facing page: A small house lives large with tall ceilings, skylights, and ample storage.

Financing an unusual project with no comparables can be difficult. We worked with a local bank that understood the community, and they found an appraiser who understood its value. We borrowed from trusting family members, and put all of our personal resources and time into our efforts. So we were relieved when the cottages sold out quickly, and grateful when our vision was received so well.

The buyers were active singles and couples, one with a 3-year-old child. Aged 40 to 65, they were a diverse group: a retired librarian, a secretary, a therapist, a computer software trainer, a graphic artist, a music teacher, a realtor, and an attorney. Almost all of them owned only one car. In the years since completion of the neighborhood in 1998, some cottages have resold with price tags of as much as 250 percent of their original price, proving their enduring value.

Third Street Cottages was our first step toward providing an alternative to the large-scale, one-size-fits-all mentality of the mainstream construction industry. That step has invigorated other architects and developers to create similar neighborhoods, and has shown the home-buying public that "sensible is better."

## A HOUSE WITH A NAME

Residents who move into the Third Street Cottages are encouraged to name their new homes, with names like *Salmonberry, Pears & Cherries,* and *Hilltop.* Each name is personal, with a story behind it.

This idea came from the place where I grew up in Minnesota. When my family settled there in the 1890s, streets had names but no address numbers. Houses were named for their character, their location, or the humor of their residents: *The Bungalow, Edgewood, Lumbago.* This last name was for the little cottage behind our house that overlooked a creek. It's a Victorian-era word given to having an aching back, or by slang, "a creek in the back."

A house with a name is not just cute, but endearing and personal. In our time, most houses are like any other, little more than a commodity that provides shelter; an investment with value in its resale. A house with a name is more likely to be a real home.

## CHAPTER 7

# A Neighborhood within a Neighborhood

We learned a lot from our experience with Third Street Cottages, where many of the key elements of designing for community came into focus. We began to understand the ramifications of innovative zoning policy on building layout and development costs. And we learned the types of finer-scale details that bring the biggest bang for the buck. That project, however, was on a small infill site in a rural town, and we wondered how our ideas for pocket neighborhoods would play out on a larger site in an established suburban neighborhood. We found our chance in Kirkland, Washington, a city just east of Seattle.

# WIKI PLANNING

Kirkland's city planners faced challenges common to most major metropolitan cities in America: how to increase the housing supply and choices for a growing population while limiting sprawl and its detrimental impact on existing neighborhoods. Taking a lesson from the creators of *Wikipedia*, they turned to the building community for creative solutions, inviting developers and architects to write their own rules. There were few guidelines, the most noteworthy being one that limited the size and type of homes. To balance this restriction, more houses would be allowed than in a standard subdivision. The catch was that the city would accept only five applications and had no obligation to approve any of them. The ones that did receive approval and were constructed would be thoroughly evaluated and considered as the basis for a new code applied generally.

Teaming again with Jim Soules and Linda Pruitt of the Cottage Company, we took on the challenge, located a piece of land, and set out to design a larger pocket neighborhood.

Danielson Grove came about through the Innovative Housing Demonstration Program of the City of Kirkland, Washington.

## Choosing the Site

The site we found was a 2¼-acre remnant of undeveloped land on a quiet street with 1960s and 1970s rambler-style homes on large lots. With land values escalating, these lots were being cut up for cul-de-sac developments of much larger houses. This site was destined to have ten 3,000-sq.-ft. houses with two- and three-car garages.

# A HOUSE FOR BETTY LU

Our initial conceptual plans for Danielson Grove were informed in part by meetings with neighboring homeowners. At the initial meeting, an elderly woman who had been a long-time local resident expressed her frustration with America's current housing stock. "My house is 2,800 sq. ft. on a ¾-acre lot. It's more than I can care for and my daughter wants me to move out. I don't want to move to an assisted living center, and I don't like condos. And you developers build houses that are too big for me. I don't have any options." We described our approach with small houses in a community setting and tried to assure her that we would work to accommodate her needs. We ended up designing a 700-sq.-ft., single-level, one-bedroom cottage with her in mind, and named it after her: "Betty Lu." We also designed a larger version with two bedrooms, named "Betty Lu Lu."

Our approach was to offer a variety cottages and houses—none larger than 1,500 sq. ft. to qualify for the density bonus—for singles, couples, and small households with children. The large-house market was glutted; we intended to cater to people who wanted a smaller home with lower maintenance and energy costs.

Above: Groves of mature fir and hemlock trees were preserved and integrated into the plan, providing instant maturity to the new neighborhood. They are also one of the key features to retaining storm-water runoff.

Right: The "Betty Lu" cottage is a 700-sq.-ft. single-level cottage designed for one or two people.

74

# CONNECTED CLUSTERS OF NEIGHBORS

Even a thoughtful selection of housing options needs an appropriate framework in which to be placed, as well as a manageable number of dwellings so as not to overwhelm the physical limitations and social requirements of the site. The Third Street Cottages had 8 households surrounding a shared courtyard. We felt that the upper limit of houses in a cluster might be about 12, which seemed to be the highest number of neighbors a person is likely to see and interact with every day, and be able to call on in an emergency. This reasoning guided us to form two clusters of homes, 16 in all, connected to each other by a walkway through a grove of trees.

Danielson Grove has two connected clusters of single-family homes and cottages connected by a walkway through a grove of trees. A new public street passes between the two as it links with a side street.

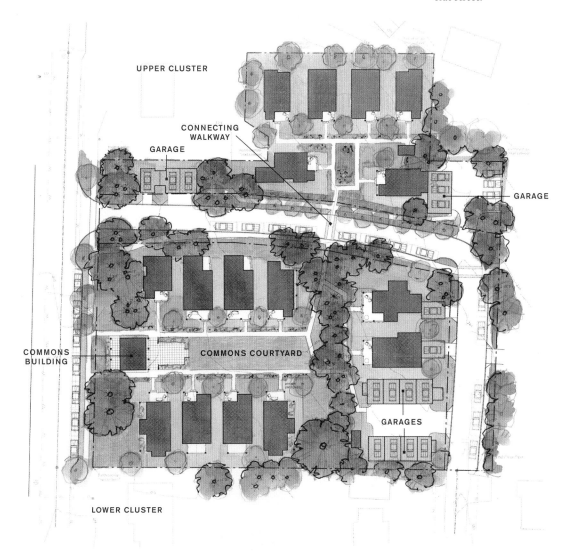

UPPER CLUSTER

CONNECTING WALKWAY

GARAGE

GARAGE

COMMONS BUILDING

COMMONS COURTYARD

GARAGES

LOWER CLUSTER

The lower courtyard is more formal in nature, with a central lawn and a flagpole; the upper courtyard has a relaxed mix of perennial flowers and shrubs.

The two courtyards have different qualities. The lower courtyard is more formal, with steeply pitched bungalow cottages lined up along the central lawn; the upper court is smaller and oriented around an informal, landscaped garden.

Garages are clustered together a short distance from the homes, an arrangement that has residents walking through the commons to their front door, offering a chance to enjoy the flowers or chat with a neighbor. This configuration also gave us the flexibility to fit buildings onto the land in ways that preserved trees and open space.

Right: Residents walk through the commons to their front doors—a daily activity that fosters interaction among neighbors. Some residents use wagons to cart groceries from their garages.

Below: Garages are clustered to the side—off the street, yet within a close walk to the houses.

A narrow, connecting local access street greatly improved the neighborhood's walkability.

# WEB OF WALKABILITY

Danielson Grove offers a network of connected walkways and local streets—a web of walkability, if you will, which reflects its livability. A good portion of its value comes from its pedestrian-friendly spaces that invite quiet, nonmotorized movement. But that walkability didn't exist at first. On our adopted street there were no sidewalks, and the street on the next block came to a dead end at the back of the property, blocking a pedestrian linkage. Our first effort, then, was to improve the neighborhood's walkability with a plan for a connecting local access street and public sidewalks along the streets bordering the property. We also planned walkways extending down the street in both directions.

We recognized four types of walking ways in a neighborhood. In addition to public sidewalks serving the surrounding community, private walks weave through the shared common areas and individual walks lead to the houses. A fourth type of walking way, which we didn't utilize in Danielson Grove, is a shared-use local street where traffic is minimal and speeds are consistently slow.

"Sustainability" and "green" are well-used terms in building construction, referring to components such as advanced framing, structural insulated panels, air-sealed envelopes, high-efficiency appliances, and low-VOC paints. Less well known, however, are "low-impact development" practices related to protecting water quality and managing storm-water runoff.

The approach is based on imitating the processes in a natural environment. For example, nearly all rainfall in a mature forest is dispersed along the forest floor, where it infiltrates into the ground, is taken up by the roots of plants and trees, or evaporates. In a built environment, where buildings, roads, parking, and lawns dominate, rainfall becomes storm-water runoff, carrying pollutants downstream. Much less water is infiltrated and taken up by roots, less evaporates, and much more becomes surface runoff.

Low-impact development practices include the following:

- preserving trees and native soils
- reducing road surface area with narrower streets
- utilizing permeable concrete and grass-paving systems for walkways, driveways, and parking areas
- directing runoff into vegetated infiltration swales (sometimes called rain gardens)
- collecting rooftop rainwater in cisterns for later use as landscape irrigation
- planting the rooftops with vegetation (known as *green roofs* or *eco-roofs)*
- amending the soil with compost
- reducing or eliminating use of pesticides

The walkways under the drip line of the trees are made of pervious concrete, which allows rainwater to infiltrate the ground directly. This was one of many strategies taken at Danielson Grove to achieve certification by the Built Green Washington program.

Storm water from roofs is directed into rain gardens—small vegetated swales alongside most homes—part of a "low-impact development" program to protect the region's salmon streams. Any rainwater that is not infiltrated is emptied into yard drains and piped to a detention vault under the Commons Building. From there it is slowly released into the city storm-water system.

## LAYERS OF PERSONAL SPACE

PRIVATE

BR

LR  K

PRIVATE
YARD

DR

PERENNIAL
BORDER

LOW FENCE

SIDEWALK

COMMONS

PUBLIC

COVERED
PORCH WITH
RAILING AND
FLOWERBOX

80

Personal space is a felt sense of comfort and safety that varies from one person to another. Davy Crockett, for example, moved his cabin to the edge of the frontier when a neighbor settled within an hour's ride by horse. In many parts of the world, whole families crowd into a small dwelling, separated from the next family by only a thin wall.

This zone of personal space is measured not so much by distance as by visual and acoustic separation. Cultural and personality differences play their part, but just as important is how and where the boundaries of personal space are defined. Left undefined, a person may feel invaded. If the boundary around personal space is too enclosed, a person may feel isolated. Finding the right balance is key to cultivating community.

A pocket neighborhood has a central space defined by the cluster of houses surrounding it. Passing through the entry gate, a resident will feel a sense of arriving home, an invited guest will feel welcomed, and a stranger will feel they've crossed into private territory. This is the first layer of personal space.

In our pocket neighborhoods, we work to create five additional layers of personal space between the courtyard and the front door: a border of perennial plantings at the edge of the sidewalk; a low fence; the private front yard; the frame of the covered porch with a low, "perchable" railing and a band of flowerboxes; and the porch itself. These occur within a span of about 18 ft.

A sequence of increasingly private personal spaces continues inside the house, with active spaces located toward the front and private spaces placed farther back and upstairs.

Between the sidewalk and the front door are five layers of personal space that help balance the connection between public and private—all within a space of about 18 ft.

At the back of the homes that meet the side street, careful layering helps buffer the private space of the house and yard from the sidewalk and street.

# FRONT-SIDE/BACK-SIDE PUZZLE

The Commons Building has a face to the street in a gesture that adds interest and respect to the surrounding neighborhood.

It's easy for a courtyard community to focus inward. A more difficult challenge is to design one that relates to the surrounding community as well, without turning an unsightly back side to the street. It's a puzzle game, fitting front side and back side and accommodating the public space realm and private space appropriately.

In a typical suburban subdivision, the front sides of houses sport an impressive portico and imposing garage doors. Windows of formal, seldom-used living rooms look out onto manicured front lawns, whereas the back sides are reserved for the life of the family, with a barbeque, play area, and, in upscale areas, a swimming pool. The problem with this configuration is that it strips the street of life.

## THE COMMONS BUILDING

The focal center of the community is the Commons Building, an indoor space with adjacent outdoor terraces where residents gather for potlucks, meetings, and card games. One teenage resident invites her friends over to the space for "homework evenings." Another homeowner brings her office team over for big-picture strategy meetings. During late summer evenings, residents lay out blankets on the lawn to watch classic movies projected onto a sheet hung from the porch—popcorn included.

The Commons Building has a "front door" to the street as a friendly, neighborly gesture. On the courtyard side, double doors open to a large terrace with café tables, inviting residents to gather. The interior is simple: space for about two dozen people to sit, a counter with a sink, and a storage room for tables and chairs. In the corner, a gas-fired stove provides radiant heat.

Because there's a common space to gather, the living rooms of the individual houses have no need to be oversize to handle the occasional family reunion and large party.

The Commons Building is host to community potluck dinners, meetings, card games, movie nights, and homework evenings.

Traditional neighborhoods work well because they have large front porches facing the street, with garages accessed from the rear. The street becomes the shared commons of the neighborhood. At Danielson Grove, the front houses have windows with an outlook to the street, even as their main living spaces and porches are oriented to the courtyard. The Commons Building, as well, has a welcoming face on the public side, and its main orientation is onto the shared commons on the other side. The courtyard retains an opening into it from the street, making the streetscape interesting for passersby. Garages are accessed off of the side street (there are no driveways along the front street). Where the back, private sides of homes meet the side street, a layering of landscape and fences buffers the transition. These are some of the ways that the pieces of the public/private, front-side/back-side puzzle fit together.

The covered door facing the street adds to the sense of welcome.

# LOOKING TO THE FUTURE

Danielson Grove was one of two projects accepted by the City of Kirkland under its Innovative Housing Demonstration Ordinance. Upon completion, the city's planning department followed up with an extensive evaluation to determine whether the regulations demonstrated should be permanently adopted citywide. The study found that it provided welcome and needed alternatives to the large homes being built, in ways that integrated well with the surrounding community. Because the homes were smaller, there was not a perception of higher density, nor was there any noticeable increase in traffic. In the end, the city adopted most of the standards we proposed into a new innovative housing zoning code.

Even with its success and the precedent-setting ordinance that grew from its creation, Danielson Grove should not be viewed as an example of beauty created by rules alone. Zoning regulations and codes should never be the sole means by which the creation of vibrant neighborhoods is attempted. We may look to policy to shape our communities, but in the end, success will come through thoughtful, individual actions connecting and contributing to the common space shared with neighbors.

## CHAPTER 8

# A Pocket Neighborhood on a Challenging Site

It's no surprise that the best building sites for residential development are chosen first, leaving the most challenging and least desirable sites for last. These leftover parcels are often the only sites available in North American cities today. In these locations, the conventional cul-de-sac strategy does not always fit, but a pocket neighborhood approach with smaller houses and remote parking can offer flexibility to make a site viable for development. Such was the case for Conover Commons in Redmond, Washington.

Conover Commons fits two clusters of homes, shared open space, and parking onto a tight site.

From a developer's point of view, the Conover site was challenging. Steep slopes and a connected wetland encumbered half the 9-acre property, and the remaining half was too narrow for garage-fronted, single-family homes on a standard street.

I walked the land with developers Jim Soules and Linda Pruitt, and we saw the steep ravine and wetland as an asset rather than a liability—a quiet woodland preserve in a bustling region. Working with Redmond's Innovative Housing Demonstration Program, which gave incentives for developing size-limited and community-oriented homes, we were able to build 25 homes bordering a permanently preserved "native growth protection area."

The homes are laid out in two connected pocket neighborhood clusters, with parking gathered to the side and tucked under a few of the houses. The upper group has 12 cottages, each about 1,000 sq. ft. in size, oriented around a central green. The lower group includes 13 larger homes, ranging in size from 1,100 sq. ft. to 2,400 sq. ft., some with a walk-out lower level and an affordable apartment above a garage, arranged along a garden walkway with a smaller open lawn. This variety of home sizes and types attracted a variety of households, from working and retired singles and couples to young families.

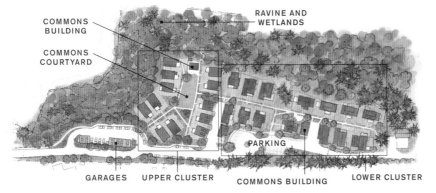

A steep ravine and protected wetlands created strict boundaries on where development could occur on this site. A pocket neighborhood with remote parking offered more flexibility than a conventional cul-de-sac subdivision on the remaining buildable area.

The lower group of homes fronts onto a garden walkway and looks onto the forested ravine on the back side.

# KEEPING THE CARS AT BAY

It was virtually impossible to have car access to all of the houses on this site, but we saw this as a selling point rather than a shortcoming. Too often, cars dominate a neighborhood, with overly wide streets that encourage speeding and expanses of driveways and garage doors that command the entrances. Most interactions among neighbors occur in front of their homes, so limiting the intrusion of cars into this space allows neighbors to engage more easily with one another.

Conover resident Wilma Manchester agrees. "I like that there are no cars in front of our house, or traffic noise, or big blank garage doors. I'm much more likely to talk with my neighbor across the way without a street between us. And, it's more peaceful here without cars in front."

The upper cluster of cottages is gathered around an open lawn.

86

Coming around the end of the garage at the drive into Conover, guests are greeted with a parking spot and the entrance into the commons—not a wall of in-your-face garage doors. Yet with another quarter turn, homeowners have easy access to their garage. Parking is accessible, but not dominant. Farther down the lane, other residents park under a set of houses or tuck into a pocket of garages and walk through the commons to their front doors.

One of the two required parking spaces for each home is "undesignated." This means that when a resident is at work or on vacation, or if a household has only one car, the second space is available for anyone to use. The result is more efficient use of the parking spaces, with less chance for overflow into the surrounding neighborhood.

Above left: Guests are greeted with a parking spot near the entry, not a wall of garage doors.

Above right: Residents park their cars in a garage to the side, or tucked under the houses, and walk through the commons to their front doors. Rather than being considered a hardship, most residents appreciate the opportunity to enjoy the gardens along the way and chat with a neighbor—in addition to not having cars and traffic noise out front.

87

Above the garage, in line with the entry walk, a second-floor commons room is used for exercise and watching movies.

Above: Some of the trees taken down on the property were milled into structural timber and paneling for use in the Commons Building.

Below: Extending out into the ravine beyond the Commons Building, an overlook platform has a tree-house-like vantage.

# A SHARED COMMONS BRINGS PEOPLE TOGETHER

Conover Commons is all about connections: between nature and people, and among its residents. One of the key elements that encourages this connectivity is the Commons Building. "A Commons Building is a requirement as far as I'm concerned," says Jim Soules. "It doesn't need to be an architectural masterpiece, but location is important. Placing it at the far end of a neighborhood, without any focus, and without people walking by it on a daily basis is asking that it not be used."

In a best-case scenario, the Commons Building should function as an extension of everyone's living room: a larger space to gather for family events and neighborhood get-togethers. At Conover Commons, all of this is happening, and more. On Thursday mornings several residents regularly meet for knitting, sewing projects, computer work, or sorting pictures; two evenings are reserved for yoga; and there are often scheduled and spontaneous potlucks and suppers.

The building was constructed with fir trees taken down on the property and used for structural timbers, beams, and paneling. Doors open wide to the south lawn, and a wall of windows on the opposite side opens to the forested ravine. There is one main room—large enough for everyone in the upper cluster of cottages—with a counter and sink, a storage room, and a toilet room accessed from the back deck. Solar photovoltaic panels on the roof supply all its electricity needs, as well as the outside yard lights for the cottages.

The shared commons draws neighbors together for potlucks, garden work parties, and movie nights.

Opposite the Commons Building, in line with the entry walk, is the end of the garage. I was adamant that such a strong axis should not be focused on a garage door, so I suggested a second-floor room with a hipped-roof and wrap-around windows. We didn't have a specific use figured out for this space, but after the residents moved in, several people brought their exercise equipment up there, along with a big TV and couches for movie nights. "It could well be it's the most used space in the community," says one resident. In a list of shared facilities for a pocket neighborhood, a common tool shed should be right near the top. "Since most people are willing to share garden tools," says Linda Pruitt, "a few sets of each tool are all that's needed. After all, how many rakes, shovels, hoes, and lawn mowers do you need in a close-knit neighborhood?"

The Commons Building at Conover opens to the south lawn on one side and the forested ravine on the other side.

"Our cottages can hold six or eight people for dinner, so when we have a larger gathering of visiting relatives, we meet in the Commons Building. It works!"

—CONOVER RESIDENT

The commons is the glue that brings people together in a pocket neighborhood. Caring for the commons, however, can stress relationships between otherwise friendly neighbors—especially if they come with unrealistic expectations or operate from a lack of knowledge of how pocket neighborhoods function.

For some, the tasks of tending the gardens, mowing the lawn, and cleaning the Commons Building is joyful work. But for others, these chores are burdens on busy schedules, adding stress and sparking feelings of guilt when left undone.

"Many people assume the commons is a mythical pea-patch—everyone working together and using it fully," says developer Jim Soules. "In practice, this doesn't happen. Some people use it a lot, others not at all. Some take care of it, others not. People take part in unequal shares—that's human nature."

Caring for a shared commons requires an equal balance of stepping forward and letting be, balancing the need to get the work done with a tolerant, informal atmosphere that allows everyone to relax and enjoy its natural beauty.

"The lesson we've learned," says Soules, "is not to expect people to contribute their time equally. So, we set up homeowner's dues to include some professional maintenance of the commons, and have the residents change it on their initiative if they want to do more work themselves."

# AN INTEGRAL LANDSCAPE

On the one hand, landscape can serve as decoration, as an appliqué to make a building look prettier. But on the other hand, landscape can be integral with building forms, woven so that both reinforce one another, like a children's book in which the writing and images work together to tell the story. Rather than pictures merely illustrating the writing, they are an integral aspect of the design, telling a part of the story in ways that words cannot.

Although the form and shape of a house are static, plantings change with the seasons and years, enlivening the life of our surroundings. At Conover Commons, tall, fully grown fir, cedar, hemlock, and maple trees set the stage and backdrop for the buildings. These mature trees change very slowly—in time spans of decades or generations—so we didn't lightly remove them unless they could not be integrated into the plan. We introduced native small trees and woody shrubs—including mountain spruce, vine maple, rhododendron, Oregon grape, and rosa rugosa—to provide a core structure of the landscape at a smaller scale. These plants change, but relatively slowly over time. Set against the backdrop of these structural plantings are the soft perennials and annuals such as geranium, primrose, and rudbeckia. These grow quickly, offering accent, aroma, and color. Finally, at the center we have a quiet lawn to balance all the richness that surrounds it.

"The garden is a life force. People feel this. When I asked the home-owners what they value most—gardens were Number 1, right up there with the houses themselves. This is a tremendous asset."
—LINDA PRUITT, DEVELOPER

## CHAPTER 9

# The Neighborhood the Neighbors Built

When Mary Sweet's name was picked in an affordable housing lottery, her prize was as precious as money. She won an opportunity to own a home in upscale Boulder, Colorado, where housing prices had skyrocketed beyond her reach. The deal was that she had to work with her future neighbors to build the house from the ground up, literally sawing studs, swinging a hammer, and raising walls. "We were nurses, teachers, artists, and professionals, and we built all the cottages, working in teams every Saturday from 8 a.m. until dark."

The 14 homes in the Poplar Community were completed in 1996 through the initiative of the Affordable Housing Alliance, formed by architects John Wolff and Tom Lyon along with attorney Matt Cohn. Their goal was to create ownership opportunities for low-income families willing to contribute sweat equity. "Ownership is empowering," Wolff says, "and this approach opens the door for more people to achieve that goal." The site is laid out with two front houses flanking an entry gate off the street. A narrow walkway opens to a grassy courtyard surrounded by gabled houses with front porches. Residents have automobile access to their homes from an alley that surrounds the perimeter of the parcel. Parking spots are off of the alley, though residents enter their homes from the courtyard side—an approach that encourages interaction among neighbors.

Some of the residents in the surrounding neighborhood were leery at first that an affordable housing "project" might devalue their homes. At 900 sq. ft., the houses at Poplar were far smaller than typical new homes, even with 500-sq.-ft. finished basements. But neighbors' concerns have proven unfounded. The 1¾-story cottages with porches and traditional trim reflect Boulder's vernacular bungalows and have been maintained with pride. Sweet adds, "I'd guess that most people going by have no idea this is affordable housing."

Resale of the homes is limited to no more than 3 percent per year, ensuring affordability over the long term. That is, if the owners are willing to part with them. Over the years, only three of the cottages have changed hands. Ryan and Sam Bass, with their two pre-school-age children, are the most recent new owners, moving from Maine for a job in Boulder. "We rented in the neighborhood because we couldn't afford a house on the open market," says Ryan. "We lucked out! It's a real community, and a wonderful world for our children, who can run out our front gate, visit neighbors, and play with other kids here."

Above: The original homeowners of the Poplar Community contributed "sweat equity" in the construction of their homes as a way of being able to live in affordable housing.

Below: Fourteen homes open onto a central landscaped courtyard on a 1.4-acre site. Guests enter through a gate on the street, and residents access their homes by car along a perimeter alleyway.

93

## A PLAN FOR THE NEIGHBORHOOD

Before starting the Poplar neighborhood, the architects took inspiration from Christopher Alexander's *A Pattern Language* approach and assembled a set of design patterns to guide their planning.

**Sense of Community and Place.** Design the site and arrange the buildings to encourage neighborly interaction and public life.

**Green at the Heart.** Locate a shared garden in the center, with all the houses looking on. Give it shape to create several activity areas, some for children's play, some for quiet observation. Provide shielded lighting to promote a sense of warmth and security.

**Sense of Arrival.** Accentuate the threshold between the public street and semi-public green by narrowing the entranceway.

**Hierarchy of Public to Private Space.** Create a sequence of spaces from most private (interior living space, front porch, and entry) to semi-public (shared garden and neighborhood promenade) to public (sidewalk and street).

**Maximum Usability.** Arrange the house and adjacent outdoor spaces to make the most of a small lot, with little or no leftover space.

Above and below: Guests enter from the street via a narrowed walkway opening to the shared green beyond.

94

The central green is "held" by all that surrounds it.

**Front Porch.** Give each home a generous front porch with a raised entry, large enough to function as an outdoor living room. Place them so they're visible from the green.

**Positive Outdoor Space.** Shape the green and all private outdoor areas, large and small, to have a quality of containment and holding. The edges of these spaces can be building faces, fences, hedges, and trees.

**Storage Building.** To address the need for storing possessions such as outdoor furniture, barbeques, snow tires, and so on, provide a storage building for each household, placed to help shape positive outdoor space and screen the car from the green.

**Simple Building Forms.** Make the building design simple and straightforward so it will be not too expensive to build and so that ordinary people can help with its construction. At the same time, look for opportunities to make each building special: a window seat, a unique dormer shape, or a roof ornament.

**Parking in Back.** Locate automobile parking out of sight to the rear of the dwellings, with entrance to the homes from the courtyard side.

95

All cottages have a front porch facing the green.

# CHAPTER 10

# A Floating Neighborhood

Like many other residents of Sausalito's houseboat community, Larry Clinton moved onto a floating home for a short stay and never left. "I can't imagine living anywhere else now," he says. After more than 25 years tied up to a dock in a bay north of San Francisco, he's become the designated historian of this colorful enclave.

Houseboat communities are quintessential pocket neighborhoods, with a limited number of residences gathered around a shared commons. In this case,

the commons is a dock. And although a commons doesn't necessarily have to be a garden, a stroll down some docks could be the highlight of a garden tour. Containers of every size are filled with fruit trees, vines, and flowers, lining both sides of the dock and festooning houseboat decks and roofs. Zealous gardeners take every opportunity to place patches of soil as surrogates for land. It's not that houseboat owners long for land. To the contrary, says Clinton, "We've all got a little salt water in our veins."

## A COLORFUL COMMUNITY

A floating community can attract an unconventional group of individuals. Its unique lifestyle tends toward two extremes: introverts seeking a private refuge and gregarious types who enjoy the chat and spontaneity of conversation along the dock. Alone or together, there seems to be room for all. "If you want company," says one resident, "leave your door open and it's a sign to stop in. Close it and people leave you alone." Some docks are prone to "dock alerts": When the clouds part and the sun comes out, someone calls out for an impromptu gathering and neighbors emerge with leftovers and a bottle of wine. All together, they are like an informal, Bohemian club.

Houseboat communities are quintessential pocket neighborhoods: clusters of nearby neighbors gathered around a shared commons. Living offshore is no excuse for living without plants. Owners of floating homes take every opportunity to fill containers of every size with trees, vines, and flowers.

One of the guards at the gate.

The community evolved from a ragtag anchorage in the bay beginning in the late 1800s. It was an odd assortment, "From duck hunting cabins to elegantly upholstered retreats," Clinton reports, "including one made of abandoned streetcars on a raft." After the 1906 San Francisco earthquake and fire, many vessels became emergency shelters for families whose homes were destroyed. During World War II, thousands of men and women flooded the area to work in the nearby shipyards, creating a serious housing shortage. Anything that could float was made into living quarters.

During the 1950s the community attracted the first generation of countercultural figures, including Zen philosopher Alan Watts and painter Jean Varda. "As well as an oddball mix of folks seeking truth, enlightenment, and a free crash pad," says Clinton. The young hippies of the 1960s made many of their living quarters into "fantastical works of art," or as another describes it, "wood butchery." Since that time, numerous cultural creatives have had the Sausalito docks as their address, including entrepreneur and writer Paul Hawken, Stewart Brand of the Whole Earth Catalogs, and astronaut Rusty Schwickert.

What was once a low-cost housing alternative has become gentrified. As the hippies had feared, a mix of middle-class professionals and retirees has become the predominant population. Long-time residents felt the community had become yuppified when cable TV was installed.

98

This wonky houseboat was cobbled together from an old train car.

# BRINGING THE COMMUNITY TOGETHER

In its transition from margin to mainstream, an ongoing quandary has been how to bring sewer, water, and fire-fighting connections to the docks without evicting low/no-income people from their homes. With Sausalito's extremely expensive housing, the houseboats represent a large proportion of affordable housing. At one of the docks, the Gates Coop, agreements are being put into place where sales are off-limits to speculators. When a houseboat sells, it is passed on to other low-income qualified buyers.

Even with docks coming into safety compliance, residents do not pass off full responsibility to public first responders. "Living 8 ft. apart in boats of wood, a fire on one houseboat can quickly spread to others," says Clinton. "We have the best chance of stopping it ourselves. And if a person is having a heart attack, he or she needs immediate assistance." Neighbors are ever alert with an ear out and a nose to the wind. They practice fire drills and have training in emergency response. "The upside is that this has brought the community together. There is a lot of cohesiveness. Even though we leave each other alone, we're a tight group." What originally draws residents may be the romance of living on the water, but what seems to keep them there is the community.

The Sausalito houseboat community has been home to generations of creative people. Here, Larry Clinton enjoys a good laugh with artist friend Jim Woessner in his floating studio.

## CHAPTER 11

# Lanes, Woonerfs, and Mental Speed Bumps

Most pocket neighborhoods have a shared commons at their heart where cars are not allowed—a secluded green that's a quiet oasis and a safe world for children to play in. But banning cars from the commons isn't necessarily a defining requirement of a pocket neighborhood. The examples in this chapter show clusters of homes gathered around pedestrian spaces that are successfully and safely shared with cars.

# LANES

I had to drive around the block several times to find this tiny lane in Pasadena. Unmarked, and right off a busy street, it doesn't appear to be a public way at all, but rather a driveway to an individual house. Through a simple bend in the lane, all views beyond the first house are cut off, leaving an enclave of houses to themselves. Stepping around the curve, noisy sounds of traffic drop away to bird songs and muffled voices coming from the houses.

About a dozen homes nestle up to the narrow access road, which seems friendlier to pedestrians and children than cars. Or strangers. Without an invitation, I feel a bit like a stranger in someone's private yard—a clear sign of being in a pocket neighborhood. Within a few minutes, one of the residents steps out to ask if I need any help, whereby we engage in conversation about the lane, stories of raising children, and summer projects. I even get a personal tour of his house. A stranger becomes a welcome guest.

The scale and character of this lane is decidedly European. Tan and cream-colored stucco walls with arched arcades front directly onto the lane on both sides, framing a proportion more vertical than broad. Balconies with ornamented brackets reach into the narrow passage. A recessed porch with draped curtains steps directly onto the lane. Tall garden walls with enticing gates hide private yards behind, scented with bougainvillea and lemon trees. It's a treat for the senses.

Above: Off of a busy street and around a curve, a dozen homes open onto a quiet pedestrian lane in Pasadena, California. Cars are welcome, but only at a walking pace.

101

Above: A recessed porch becomes a summer living room.

Left: Balconies, porches, and arcades open directly onto this lane, conveying a sense of territoriality felt both by strangers and welcomed guests.

## WOONERFS

Although a lane is a narrow road for cars that is easily shared with pedestrians, a "woonerf" is a pedestrian space reluctantly shared with cars. The term is a Dutch word that roughly translates as "living street." It originated in the Netherlands as a place where pedestrians, bicyclists, playing children, and even casual loiterers have reign over the whole street. Motorized traffic is allowed, but only at a walking pace.

"When you see traffic problems as a traffic problem, you will only get traffic solutions."
—HANS MONDERMAN

Woonerfs have no lane markings, curbs, sidewalks, signals, or crossing signs. They are, however, surfaced with paving blocks to signal a pedestrian zone. This contrarian approach blurs the lines between vehicular and people space. Unsure of what space belongs to them, drivers become much more alert. Jan Gehl, an urban planner from Copenhagen, finds that "people look each other in the eye and maneuver in respect." The outcome is drastically slower traffic and far fewer accidents.

102

Woonerfs are pedestrian zones where cars are allowed, but only at a walking pace.

Hans Monderman, the traffic engineer who pioneered the woonerf concept, argued that roads designed for safety—wide lanes with traffic signs, speed bumps, and separation from pedestrians—are actually less safe. "Traffic signs," Monderman contended, "are an invitation to stop thinking. They tell us, go ahead, don't worry; we've got you covered. Nothing can happen to you." With counterintuitive genius, he suggested the opposite: confusion and ambiguity. Without clear signals, signs, or boundaries, drivers are brought to heightened alertness: "Pay attention!" The result is that drivers slow way down.

## MENTAL SPEED BUMPS

David Engwicht, an artist and teacher working in Australia, made a similar discovery. He noticed that children playing along a street slowed traffic much more effectively than did speed bumps. He pushed this idea further, organizing dinner parties and social events in the street. Universally, drivers slowed way down. But rather than expressing frustration, they were curious as to what was going on.

Engwicht's view is that drivers are affected by two factors: intrigue—"What's happening here? What's the story?"—and uncertainty—"What's about to happen? Watch out!" By taking away signs and traffic control devices, intrigue and uncertainty become "mental speed bumps" that automatically slow drivers without their noticing.

> David Engwicht made a discovery that building the social life of the street is an effective way to tame traffic.

## HOW CAN A STREET BECOME A NEIGHBORHOOD COMMONS?

Local streets can become active neighborhood common spaces when residents begin to think of the street as a room and shape their properties to make the room work well as a commons. Here are a few ideas to get started:

**Connection and Contribution.** The public space is shaped by its surrounding private properties. When each building and yard makes a connection to the shared street space by its own unique contribution, the street has more vitality. This might be a colorful gable, a broad front porch, or a running hedge of perennial plantings.

**Active Spaces Looking On.** Orient at least one of the home's active rooms toward the street—a living room or a porch large enough to be lived in. These "eyes" on the commons are the first line of defense of the neighborhood's security, making the block a safer place to live.

**Layers of Personal Space.** People will more likely engage in the commons when the personal space is well defined. A sequence of layers may include the active interior space/porch/front garden/ low fence and hedge/front gate. Pay attention to getting the right balance of exposed and enclosed.

**Enclosure.** Just as conversation is more engaging when people are a certain distance apart, the life of the street will be more alive when buildings are appropriately close.

**Clear Entry and Territory.** A street will become more of a room when the entries are clearly defined. Consider narrowing the ends of the block with planting beds, arching trees, and a crosswalk to signal drivers that they are entering a residential zone.

**Shared-Use Street.** Pedestrians are an essential ingredient of the neighborhood commons. They can have the right-of-way on local streets when traffic speeds are less than 20 mph.

104

## THINK OF STREETS AS ROOMS

Streets are more than the routes we take to get somewhere else. Another way to think of them is as rooms whose walls are made of building facades, trees, hedges, and fences—rooms with a sense of enclosure that feel good to be in. When traffic slows to a walking pace, streets can also become the neighborhood commons—places where neighbors meet casually and children play, while other neighbors overlook all the activity from their porches and homes.

When local streets are thought of as rooms, as in the Barrio Santa Rosa neighborhood in Tucson, Arizona, shown here, they will more likely become the neighborhood commons. The "walls" of these rooms help create a sense of enclosure that feels good to be in. Each of the surrounding property owners can make a contribution to shaping the room: a colorful gable, a running hedge of perennial plantings, a bench or sitting area facing onto the street.

## CHAPTER 12

# Back House, Front House, Lane

Bob lives in back in a 425-sq.-ft. cottage. He likes to stay up late and sleep in. Anne lives in front across the lane in a 1,200-sq.-ft. house. She goes to bed early and wakes early. They met during midlife, fell in love, and married. Knowing themselves, they realized they wanted to share a life, but not live under the same roof. Their neighbor Joanne is a writer and uses her back house as a creative studio. Her husband John likes to tinker in the garage. They live in the front house. Marcy and Robert live in the third front house and welcome visiting friends, children, and grandchildren to stay in their back house. Three couples, three lifestyles. And between them runs a lane. "It was an experiment," says developer Jim Soules, "to show that there was a market for *duet homes*—our term for two small houses on one property. And it sets an example for another version of a pocket neighborhood."

Originally two lots on a cul-de-sac, local ordinances allowed the parcels to be subdivided into three smaller lots, each with a primary house and an "accessory dwelling unit." An easement was created for a shared lane to cross over the three properties.

The private lane functions as a shared commons for the surrounding houses and cottages. The couples have the autonomy of their own property, yet interact with each other far more than if the parcels were completely separate.

A small house with a backyard cottage offers more flexibility in use than one big house. And although the overall square footage of the buildings on the three lots may be about the same as two typical homes and garages, the smaller buildings break up the massing into a finer scale and character.

Rather than a typical cul-de-sac lined with "garage-door" houses, each household in this pocket neighborhood has a main house in front, a small cottage in back, and between them is a shared lane.

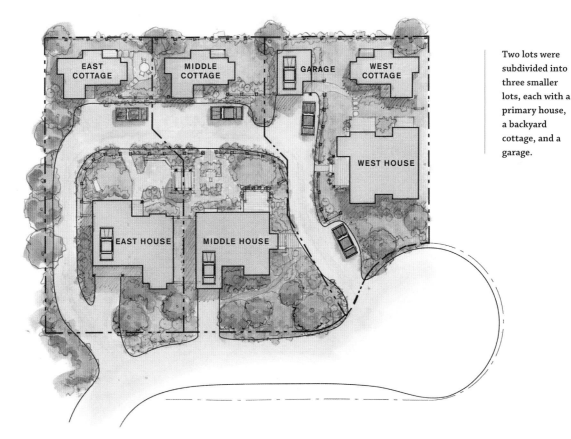

Two lots were subdivided into three smaller lots, each with a primary house, a backyard cottage, and a garage.

108

Above: The front houses have large porches with translucent roofing.

Right: Backyard cottages, a garage, and one of the front houses open to the lane. In the foreground, a two-side sitting shelter spans a property line.

## BACKYARD COTTAGES

A backyard cottage is a small, detached home on the same property as a primary single-family residence. Sometimes called "accessory dwelling units," "granny flats," "mother-in-law apartments," or "carriage houses," they are self-contained units with their own kitchens, bathrooms, bedrooms, and living spaces.

Backyard cottages are increasingly being allowed in residential zones across the country as a way to expand the supply of affordable and alternative housing opportunities. The City of Seattle allows detached cottages as large as 800 sq. ft. on lots over 4,000 sq. ft. in all city neighborhoods. "Backyard cottages are an important part of what makes Seattle livable and sustainable," says city planner Diane Sugimura. "They offer options for renters and for homeowners seeking to remain in their present homes, and help reduce the pressure for sprawl." And because of their small scale, backyard cottages can do this with minimal impact on the surrounding neighborhood.

These accessory units have a great variety of potential uses: as starter housing for young adult family members; as an alternative for an elderly homeowner to avoid the emotional and financial costs of having to move into a nursing home or assisted living facility; as close-by living quarters for a caregiver; or as a home office, art studio, or rental for supplementary income.

## CHAPTER 13

# New Urban Pocket Neighborhoods

Don't be fooled by the name, the whole notion of "New Urbanism" is relatively old. This movement among planners and architects emerged in the 1980s as a response to the ubiquitous sprawl that was spiraling out of control in the United States. Heralded by Andrés Duany and Elizabeth Plater-Zyberk with their design for the new town of Seaside, Florida, New Urbanism espouses a number of old-city principles.

First among these is "walkability"—being able to walk to a wide array of destinations in daily life, such as school, friends, shops, restaurants, and recreation areas. Walkable streets are pedestrian friendly. Roadways are designed to slow traffic and are lined by human-scale features such as buildings with porches and thoughtful detail, trees, and landscaping.

"Connectivity" is another principle—having an interconnected network of streets and sidewalks to disperse traffic and make walking more pleasurable. Other key principles include having a mix of shops, workplaces, and homes; a diversity of styles and range of prices; and all at higher densities to promote sociability and ease the pressures of sprawl. The idea is to create livable cities with a tapestry of life across a full range of scales, from a single building to an entire community.

Walkability is a key principle of New Urbanism.

## FINDING THE IN-BETWEEN SCALE

New Urbanist communities are often planned with a traditional grid of local streets and back alleys. In this layout, the street is animated with activity from slowly passing cars, people walking by on the sidewalk, and chatter from the porches. Local streets are community public spaces

After Hurricane Katrina hit the Gulf Coast, a team of New Urbanist designers brainstormed solutions for rebuilding communities. One of the first examples to be built is at Ocean Springs, Mississippi, where cottages face onto a shared green.

The grid pattern of streets and alleys in the Wellington Neighborhood is augmented with a pattern of landscaped greens spanning between parallel streets.

shaped by the flanking houses and open to the wider neighborhood in a loose flow of congenial interaction. Obviously missing from most New Urbanist plans, however, is the semi-public space *without cars*. There can be lovely individual houses on very livable blocks, but the in-between scale of a pocket neighborhood—a shared commons held by a cluster of houses—is rarely seen.

## Wellington Neighborhood

New Urbanist neighborhoods that work at the in-between scale do exist, however. An example is the shared community greens of the Wellington Neighborhood in Breckenridge, Colorado, designed by Wolff + Lyon Architects.

The neighborhood is arranged on a grid pattern of local streets and alleys, but rather than homes fronting directly onto the street, clusters of 8 to 12 homes face onto a landscaped green spanning perpendicularly between two streets. Residents park their cars off of an alley to the rear, and guests use parking pockets along the street and approach the homes through the commons. The ends of the greens are "pinched" to heighten the sense of a gateway and shared territory among residents.

The Waters, Alabama: Pocket neighborhood greens within New Urban communities pull together clusters of nearby neighbors and connect to the wider neighborhood through a network of sideways and footpaths.

112

## New Town at St. Charles

This New Urban neighborhood in Missouri is in the process of becoming a full-fledged town, with five pedestrian-friendly districts, each with a distinct park serving that neighborhood. At its core is a commercial, civic, and cultural center. Here and there are smaller pocket greens spanning between two streets and shared by a half dozen houses. "Our porch opens to a little park, not parking," says architect Tim Bussey, who lives on one such green. "It's our own sub-neighborhood within the larger neighborhood."

> "Pocket neighborhoods are a perfect fit with New Urbanism because of their fine-grained nature."
> —STEVE MOUZON, TOWN ARCHITECT OF THE WATERS

## The Waters

This New Urbanist town in Alabama is planned for 2,500 homes and a small commercial district. Within the community is a cluster of 10 two-story houses that nestle around a small green, creating an intimate shared commons. Cars are sequestered to the rear alley, and deep porches spill onto a quiet lawn on the courtyard side.

Cottages face onto a shared green at New Town at St. Charles.

## FACE THE STREET

The main staple of the housing industry has traditionally been the "rear-view" house. Facing away from the street, it offers occupants a view of a golf course, a wetland preserve, or at least a private backyard. The street side is left with the garage door, arched portico, and a living room window: formal and presentable, yet offering little more than a blank smile.

Above: Rear-view houses shun the street, looking the other way. Front-loaded garages leave the front face blank and offer nothing to the life of the street.

Right: Houses facing the street bring life to the street with active rooms, porches, and steps.

New Urbanism offers many lessons about bringing life to the street. More than just an access way for cars and services, the street can be a public "room," a shared place to see and engage with neighbors and passersby. The street is brought alive by facing active rooms, porches, and broad steps of a house toward the street and parking cars off of a rear alley. In existing plats without alleys, limit the garage and driveway to no more than a third of the front face, slipping the parking alongside or in back.

# COURTYARD HOUSING

Courtyard housing is another variation of the New Urbanist theme. New Urban suburban communities typically have 3 to 5 houses per acre of land. If single-family homes were the only alternative, communities would continue to sprawl, highways would be jammed even more than they are, and many people would be at a loss for appropriate housing. New Urbanists promote building at higher densities to limit sprawl, create housing options, and increase walkability. One such option is courtyard housing, which has a density of 25 to 30 dwellings per acre.

**Private apartments with windows and balconies look out onto a shared courtyard at Harper Court: Seven Fountains in West Hollywood, California. The complex features 20 units wrapped around 4 courtyards.**

Meridian Court has 10 townhouses oriented around a common courtyard on a 0.4-acre site, which translates to a density of 25 dwellings per acre.

## Meridian Court

Picking up on a rich tradition of courtyard housing in southern California (see pp. 44–49), architects and planners Stephanos Polyzoides and Elizabeth Moule designed and built Meridian Court in Pasadena. Located a short walk away from a regional light rail and commercial district, this infill project emulates the New Urbanist principles of connectivity, mixed uses, and walkability.

Meridian Court was built as a demonstration project to show how higher-density housing can fit into a community. "The rules of courtyard housing are very simple," says Polyzoides. "You walk through an open passage off the street and have direct access to the individual units from the courtyard. All parking is underground. Apartments facing the street have front doors onto the street." Meridian features 10 townhouses around a common courtyard, each with its own private patio. Parking is tucked under the building, accessed from a diminutive driveway on the side. There are no corridors, balconies, or elevators, saving costs over stacked apartments of the same density. "The courtyard model," says Polyzoides, "builds on a friendly scale and provides an extremely high level of livability because of its natural light, cross-ventilation, and the gardens."

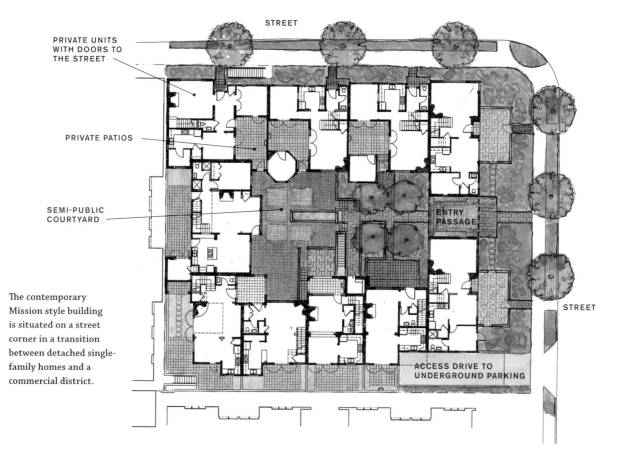

PRIVATE UNITS
WITH DOORS TO
THE STREET

PRIVATE PATIOS

SEMI-PUBLIC
COURTYARD

STREET

ENTRY
PASSAGE

STREET

ACCESS DRIVE TO
UNDERGROUND PARKING

The contemporary Mission style building is situated on a street corner in a transition between detached single-family homes and a commercial district.

The view into the court from just inside the passage.

## WHAT MAKES A NEIGHBORHOOD "REAL"?

One criticism sometimes leveled at New Urbanism is that it does not tolerate messiness. In efforts to counteract car-centered suburban sprawl, New Urban planners prescribe elaborate codes to create human-scale, walkable communities, and developers set restrictive covenants to protect their look and lifestyle. These new towns, however, can sometimes feel a bit like Jim Carrey's idyllic but illusionary town of Seahaven in the movie, *The Truman Show*. Perfect, but not real.

Ironically, many New Urbanists are inspired by Jane Jacobs's passionate description of the mosaic of apartments, shops, and vendors on her block in Greenwich Village in New York City. It was a scene of apparent disorder and mixed-up diversity that she vehemently defended for its authenticity and life. Like the tattered Velveteen Rabbit, Jacobs's block was lived in and loved enough to achieve a state of "realness."

Whether anything new can have realness is a good question. It takes time to cultivate genuine relationships, and time to fine-tune a home and garden to one's liking. It's hard to say what makes a neighborhood real, but this quality tends to emerge from a balance of planning and improvisation, from caring for and letting be. And no doubt, realness appears in neighborhoods where neighbors know one another.

## CHAPTER 14

# Lines of Enticement

When Jeff Shelton is designing a building, he keeps his eye out for "god lines," a term he uses for the lines of enticement that make you curious to follow a path through a gate or around the next bend. He tries to find the "master line" as he begins to develop a design, and treats it almost as an animate being, tracing its path and coaxing it to reveal its special delights. "You may not be able to see these lines," he says "but you can certainly feel them."

119

Seven attached residences and a commercial space open onto a series of interlocking courtyards. Parking is tucked into garages on side and rear alleys.

Shelton worked with these design lines as he and a team of craftsmen created the Cota Street Studios in Santa Barbara, California. This pocket neighborhood of seven attached residences and one commercial space is organized around a series of interlocking courtyards—each space drawing you into the next. Like their cousins in the Mediterranean hill towns of Andalucía, Spain, the lines have the seduction of a Flamenco dancer.

Walking along the sidewalk, the bell fashioned into the front gate is what first catches your eye. You're drawn to peek into the courtyard beyond, where the sound of an unseen fountain entices you to enter. It's private, yet open; visually engaging, yet hushed. A sequence of spaces unfolds one after another, each one drawing you deeper into its world.

The outermost courtyard is located just off of a busy street in downtown Santa Barbara. The first building inside is a retail space, with large sliding doors opening into the court. From here, through a gate, is the second courtyard, with a cerulean blue glazed ceramic fountain. Another arched opening beckons entry to the third courtyard, this one with an overlooking balcony with a wrought-iron railing and colorful awning. A stair draws one up from here into the final courtyard, surrounded with potted geraniums and fragrant roses in raised planters.

"It's about life, as simple as that. Do you feel alive? More fully yourself? That's it!"
—JEFF SHELTON

Above: Architect Jeff Shelton and contractor Dan Upton work together in a collaborative process to create unique environments.

Facing page: The designer and craftsmen collaborated closely to work out the details of construction, such as this unusual double-sliding door.

## A CREATIVE PARTNERSHIP

Shelton might be able to imagine and draw spaces like this, but the delight he talks about came out during the process of construction with the creative engagement of the builders. Shelton is like a movie director, guiding the talents of the producer, actors, camera operator, editors, and support crew to create a dramatic production. To continue the metaphor, contractor Dan Upton is the producer. He was the one with the creative challenge of building Shelton's designs and making sure the intent was carried through in the final product.

Shelton would sketch an arched double-sliding door, a wavy ironwork balcony railing, and undulating stuccoed walls that are 2 ft. thick—all with a whimsical quirkiness, but drawn with precise intent. Upton pushed his crew to see what they could do. At the same time, there's a fine line with creative freedom. Shelton explains: "We ask the crew to put themselves into the building, to make it come to life. But we also ask them to leave their egos at the door." These buildings are not the place for personal statements. In subtle reference to his god lines, he says, "Each element must support the building coming to life. It must be integral. Otherwise, it's 'plop' art."

With the Cota Street Studios, Shelton worked with Upton on developing the basic construction details and drafted permit drawings with the essential structural information. Once construction began, Shelton would be on site every day to work with Upton and his crew to refine the forms and details. They would mock up tile patterns one day, then move forward the next day to construct it. "Sometimes," says Shelton, "a detail wouldn't work out as we planned. But there was no panic or blame. We'd use the opportunity to turn it into something different." In these ways, they were able to achieve an uncanny fit among all the parts.

> "It is an artistic process of weaving together connections into a whole fabric, ideally covering whole neighborhoods and all around town."
> —JEFF SHELTON

Cota Street Studios has a kind of beauty that does not come about merely by carrying out orders. It was created with a dynamic process, much like a painter goes through to arrive at a compelling composition. Shelton describes it as an artistic process of "weaving together connections into a whole fabric, ideally covering whole neighborhoods and all around town." Perhaps the fabric he is describing is woven of god lines.

Living units have an outdoor patio and look onto a courtyard shared by two or three other households. Each courtyard has its own character and quality, using a contemporary vernacular of Mission style forms and materials.

122

Tile, stucco, and ironwork come together in a play of delightful form, weaving together inside and outside spaces in a balance of connection and privacy.

123

## CHAPTER 15

# Pocket Neighborhoods within a Village

Village Homes, a community of 240 homes within 18 pocket neighborhood clusters in Davis, California, is widely considered the first "green" neighborhood in the United States. Built in the wake of the mid-1970s energy crisis on 70 acres of land in California's Central Valley, it features solar homes, an extensive network of narrow streets, pedestrian and bike paths, common areas and community gardens, edible landscaping, and an innovative natural drainage system. However cutting edge it might have seemed at the time, its designers and developers, Michael and Judy Corbett, drew directly from Ebenezer Howard's 1899 vision of garden cities and Howard Wright and Clarence Stein's 1929 garden city plan for Radburn, New Jersey (see pp. 32–43).

Like Radburn, Village Homes is a contained neighborhood of homes in smaller pocket neighborhood groupings of 8 to 16 homes around shared common areas. These clusters are served by alley-like cul-de-sacs that dovetail with pedestrian greenways leading to large public open spaces.

## ENVIRONMENTAL FOCUS

What distinguishes Corbett's plan from the Radburn plan is its environmental focus. Local streets run east to west and lots are oriented north to south, so that all the homes can make full use of solar energy. Most windows face south, with overhangs that shade summer sun and allow the low winter sun to add heat to the house. Annual household energy bills are a third to a half of those in surrounding neighborhoods, due to passive heating, natural cooling, and solar hot water systems.

The streets are narrow—23 ft. wide as opposed to a suburban standard of 36 ft.—and shaded by deciduous trees, which minimize the amount of pavement exposed to the intense summer sun.

Storm water is allowed to filter back into the ground through a system of drainage swales and ponds that run through the common areas. Compare this to a typical subdivision, where lots are graded toward the street and storm water is eliminated through an expensive network of pipes.

Curving narrow streets are shaded by deciduous trees, keeping the neighborhood cooler during hot California summers.

The 70-acre site has a series of cul-de-sac access drives coming off of a neighborhood connector street. Pocket neighborhood clusters have car access on one side, alternating with a shared green on the other, which connects to a large park, community gardens and orchards, Common Buildings, and neighborhood businesses.

125

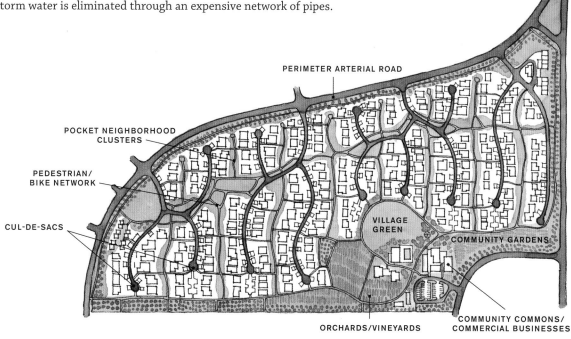

PERIMETER ARTERIAL ROAD

POCKET NEIGHBORHOOD CLUSTERS

PEDESTRIAN/ BIKE NETWORK

CUL-DE-SACS

VILLAGE GREEN

COMMUNITY GARDENS

ORCHARDS/VINEYARDS

COMMUNITY COMMONS/ COMMERCIAL BUSINESSES

Storm water filters back into the ground through drainage swales in the pocket neighborhood greens.

Fruit and nut trees and vineyards form a large element of the landscaping in the neighborhood. This edible landscape produces oranges, almonds, apricots, pears, persimmons, peaches, plums, cherries, and grapes. In the community gardens, located on the west side of the development, residents grow vegetables, fruits, flowers, and herbs for home use and sale to markets and restaurants.

Holistic approaches to environmental issues can bring unexpected benefits. "You know you're on the right track when you notice that your solution for one problem accidentally solves several other problems," Michael says. For example, in trying to conserve fossil fuels by minimizing the need for automobiles, they found that streets and parking could be minimized. Reduced asphalt lowered the ambient air temperature 10°F to 15°F compared to surrounding neighborhoods in summer months. Narrower streets also slowed traffic, which reduced noise, beautified the neighborhood, and proved safer for children.

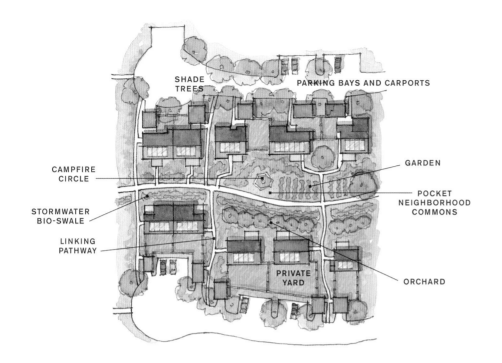

SHADE TREES

PARKING BAYS AND CARPORTS

CAMPFIRE CIRCLE

STORMWATER BIO-SWALE

LINKING PATHWAY

GARDEN

POCKET NEIGHBORHOOD COMMONS

PRIVATE YARD

ORCHARD

Within the pocket neighborhood clusters, community and privacy dovetail in a pattern of streets and neighborhood greens. Local streets are more like alleys, with parking bays and carports tucked right off the pavement. Although the connection to the house is from the street, high fences and shrubs form a private courtyard from which the cars are not visible. On the opposite side, the houses open to the central green, shared with 8 to 10 neighbors. Design guidelines prohibit fences here, but hedges and trees create a sense of privacy as needed.

# NEIGHBORHOOD PIONEERS

## JUDY CORBETT

Judy Corbett is a woman on a mission. After the challenges of getting Village Homes approved by her city, she set up the Local Government Commission (LGC) to help educate officials on social and environmental issues. "It was clear to me that without mayors and city council managers and supervisors taking the lead in making things change, Village Homes could never be duplicated," she says.

With the LGC, Corbett hosted 10 national "Smart Growth" conferences for local government officials and published more than 50 policy guidebooks on topics such as water and energy conservation, alternative energy, sustainable economic development, and resource-efficient land-use patterns. In 1991, Corbett and the LGC drew together leading-edge urban thinkers to write the "Ahwahnee Principles for Resource-Efficient Communities," which became the basis for New Urbanism.

## A NETWORK OF LANES AND WALKWAYS

Shared-use streets.

128

Village Homes is a network of walking pathways and slow streets—a pedestrian-oriented design that has residents walking on a daily basis as a part of their lives, encouraging them to stay in good health and to know their neighbors.

**Shared-Use Streets.** Because the access lanes are narrow and not through-streets, cars move slowly, allowing the streets to be safely used as walking ways and play areas as well.

**Cul-de-Sac Connection.** At the end of each lane, a pathway opens into the village commons, providing an easy walking connection to community amenities.

**Midblock Passageways.** Perpendicular to the access lanes and pocket neighborhood walkways are narrow passageways, allowing an easier walking connection between the clusters and to the adjacent street.

Cul-de-sac connection.

Midblock passageways.

**Pocket Neighborhood Walkways.** Eight to twelve houses face onto a shared greenspace, which has a footpath running through it. This, in turn, connects to wider walkways linking the clusters and the community commons.

Above: Clustered mailboxes.

Below: Ribbon walkways.

**129**

**Clustered Mailboxes.** Rather than having a mailbox at each house, residents walk to a cluster of mailboxes, creating another opportunity for neighbors to interact with one another.

**Ribbon Walkways.** Ribbons of walkways—8 ft. to 10 ft. wide—wind through and around the entire neighborhood and connect to the surrounding community.

**Gathering Spots.** Every path needs a destination, and a shady spot to sit with friends can be a pleasure.

| Gathering spots.

# A CHILD'S WORLD

Village Homes is a particularly nurturing environment for children to grow up in. Right out their back door is a greenspace with trees to climb and fruit to eat, play areas with sand and water, and ribbons of bicycle paths—an endless source of amusement and stimulation. Children can visit friends and roam throughout the community without facing the danger of crossing a street. Parents feel at ease knowing other caring adults are nearby within earshot. Rather than feeling fenced in in their backyards, the children in this community experience freedom and empowerment.

A nurturing child's world provides an endless source of amusement and stimulation within a safe environment.

## The Home Range

Given that only half of the hours of a child's waking day—and half the days of a child's year—are spent in school, the neighborhood where a child grows up is crucial in supporting that child's needs. Unfortunately, children often feel painfully isolated and lack access to places for safe, unplanned play.

What kinds of environments are safe and welcoming for children? Clare Cooper Marcus, a university professor known for her pioneering research on children's environments, claims that they should be safe enough for a child to move around independently as soon as possible. As children grow older, their boundaries should widen with them.

Cooper Marcus describes this as a need for graduated "home ranges," increasingly larger zones of play for each stage of a child's development. "If you had a baby, they would play in the room you're in. Your toddler would be free to play in the next room within earshot, provided it was 'child-proofed.' At around 3 or 4 years old, you would probably allow them to play in the backyard with friends, or in the front yard if there is a fence and gate with a latch beyond their reach, and provided you could easily see them."

For children beyond the age of about 6 years old, however, there is a gap in the graduated home range in most neighborhoods. The street out front is off-limits because of the double fear of "stranger danger" and danger from traffic. Children need to be chauffeured to friends' houses and organized sports activities. Contemporary parents, who are often working, aren't likely to say to an 8- or 10-year-old, "Why don't you run down to the park and see if there are some kids playing soccer there? You can join them."

Children have free range to roam throughout Village Homes without having to cross a street.

Children need increasingly larger zones of play for each stage of development.

## Supporting Children's Needs

Planners and neighborhood activists like to focus on walkability—the ease and friendliness of a neighborhood to pedestrians—but children in a neighborhood have their own set of needs that often go unrecognized or disregarded.

From elementary-school age, children have a real need to experience and explore the world around them spontaneously, safely, and on their own terms. They need to be able to move in wider and wider circles on their own, without having to rely on adults. This is especially true for girls beyond the age of about 8 or 9, whose home range is significantly smaller than that of boys of the same age. Cooper Marcus reports that the ability to move about independently is essential to promoting self-esteem, a sense of identity, and the capacity to be responsible.

Providing for children's needs in their neighborhoods gives them places to grow into caring, responsible adults. It works the other way around, too: Children offer opportunities for adults to be touched by their spontaneity and joy. Children are the glue that brings a community together. When their world is limited and fragmented, the glue they provide will be missing. But when they have a safe and welcoming environment that extends gradually with their abilities, we all benefit.

## THE POPSICLE INDEX

Catherine Fitts, an investment advisor, has a favorite measurement of a community's health. She calls it the Popsicle Index. This is the percentage of people in a neighborhood who think that a young child can safely walk to the neighborhood grocery and come home with a Popsicle—alone. When she was a child in Philadelphia, she believes that everybody thought that she could do that. And she did. The Popsicle Index was near 100. Now, in that same neighborhood, going alone to the grocery to buy a Popsicle isn't something many parents will allow. The Popsicle Index has collapsed to near zero.

Pocket neighborhoods offer a crucial link in widening a child's safe horizons and increasing the Popsicle Index. The shared common areas of pocket neighborhoods provide the intermediate zone where children can safely venture out and play on their own. It is a space that is somewhat private, somewhat public, and it works precisely because it's a mix of both.

# PART THREE

# COHOUSING COMMUNITIES

**There's an old African proverb that says**, "It takes a village to raise a child." Many people who live in "cohousing" communities take this sentiment to heart. Cohousing residents—not just parents with children, but people of all ages—see their neighbors as a kind of extended family. "Because we live close together and know each other well," says one cohouser, "our kids might be in any of our neighbors' houses, or roaming in packs of their friends."

Cohousing communities are pocket neighborhoods that are planned, owned, and managed by the residents themselves. These communities typically include 12 to 30 households clustered around common ground. Each home is owned privately, but residents collectively own extensive facilities, such as a kitchen and dining hall, community garden, playgrounds, offices, children's playroom, workshop, and exercise gym.

> "Not only houses for people, but also, houses by people."
> —JAN GUDMAND-HØYER, DANISH ORIGINATOR OF THE COHOUSING MODEL

Just don't call them communes. Residents insist that their housing model is different from hippie communes of the 1960s: There is no shared income, no shared religious or political beliefs, and homes are privately owned. But many of their values are similar: a desire for a more social lifestyle, environmental sustainability, and cooperative approaches to decision making and shared responsibilities.

Although its social structures may seem alternative, cohousing is gaining a foothold in mainstream culture as a viable option for living, with communities sprouting in urban, suburban, and rural settings around the world.

## CHAPTER 16

# Danish Origins

It's generally believed that cohousing originated in Denmark in the 1960s, due to the popularity of a book by American architects Kathryn McCamant and Chuck Durrett, who coined the term "cohousing." But related forms of collective housing appeared about the same time in Sweden and the Netherlands, stemming from a socially responsive tradition of shared housing throughout Northern Europe stretching back hundreds of years (see Gardens of Compassion, pp. 26–31). Nevertheless, the evolution of cohousing in Denmark offers rich examples for the study of pocket neighborhoods.

In the mid-1960s, most Danish housing options were isolated single-family houses and apartments. With many women going to work outside the home after World War II, children were left home alone. Architect Jan Gudmand-Høyer and author Bodil Graae introduced ideas for cooperative living and gathered the first groups to build a housing collective, integrating childcare and social contact. They called their approach *bofællesskab*, which translates as "living community."

The first Danish cohousing communities featured around 30 attached and detached houses, along with a Common House shared by all. Cars and parking were outside the commons, leaving a pedestrian environment that was completely safe for children.

# MANY HANDS MAKE A COMMUNITY

Cohousing has evolved from the initial Danish communities, but in all of them, resident participation is an essential ingredient.

### Participatory Design

Gudmand-Høyer felt strongly that the future residents of a community should be involved in the planning and design process from the beginning. His watchword was, "Not only houses for people, but also,

Above: Cohousing was envisioned as a community that fostered interaction among neighbors of all ages.

Below: From the very beginning, Danish cohousing communities were planned, owned, and managed by the residents themselves.

Virtually all cohousing communities gather on a weekly basis to share meals, which are prepared by rotating teams of residents.

houses by people." Although an architect can provide a vision and technical expertise, resident participation ensures that their specific needs, desires, and priorities are addressed. From all their hard work together, a feeling of pride and ownership emerges that would not happen in a typical development project. On the day they move in, a base for a strong community is already established.

## Self-Management

The spirit of participation carries over when construction is complete, as residents take part in committees to oversee all aspects of community living, from maintaining common facilities and grounds and managing budgets to organizing child care and planning social events.

## Shared Meals

Probably the one thing that defines cohousing more than any other is the shared evening meal. Plans vary among cohousing groups, but a community dinner is typically offered from two to five times a week. So, about once a month, teams of two or three will plan, prepare, and serve a meal for 40 to 70 people. That means that on all the other days of the month, you just show up. As one cohouser put it, "I'm a perennial enemy of cooking, so I'm grateful for the communal dining option. Yet when I team-cook a big meal, it's relaxing, not taxing."

# THE EVOLUTION OF COHOUSING

Danish cohousing has taken many forms since the 1960s, with individual houses grouped around courtyards, attached row houses along pedestrian lanes, rehabilitated factories and schools with covered atriums, and even high-rise buildings. The common threads to all these communities are a central pedestrian area with homes looking on, a community dining room, and cars limited to the periphery.

## Open-Air Courtyard

Drejerbanken is a community of 20 houses located in a rural village outside of the city of Odense, Denmark. It was developed in 1977 with an equal number of market-rate owner-occupied and nonprofit rental homes grouped around two courtyards. At its hub is the Common House, situated so that everyone passes it while walking from the parking area to their own houses and so that it's in view from all of the front yards. The one- and two-story attached houses are clustered, preserving space for a soccer field, common garden, and children's play area.

Drejerbanken is a classic open-air cohousing configuration, featuring two pocket neighborhood clusters to either side of a Commons Building. A central parking area is positioned so that residents walk through the commons to their homes.

## Open-Air Pedestrian Street

The layout for Trudeslund, completed in 1981 in a town just north of Copenhagen, also has a Common House at its hub, clustered parking behind, and a wooded open area. But here, 33 attached residences nestle along two well-used pedestrian streets. The Common House is located at the hub of the walkways and next to the parking area. Yet most residents use public transit and approach the community from the ends, so that the Common House is not as active as it was intended to be.

The housing cluster wings of the Trudeslund community are gathered along two active pedestrian "streets." The private side of the lower units opens to a forested common open space.

## BALANCING COMMUNITY AND PRIVACY

I n our contemporary culture, privacy is a high priority for many households. It feels good to close the door on the stresses of the outside world. Yet, the desire for a sense of community can be very strong as well. Cohousing advocates have worked to find a balance between the two.

**A Soft Edge.** Jan Gehl, a Danish urban designer, thought of the area outside the front door as a "soft edge" and considered it to be a key element in fostering interaction among neighbors. Like a front porch, this is a semi-private area that is easily accessible from inside and a comfortable place to be outside. It's likely to be defined by a different paving surface, a low fence, or a hedge, and it is where residents set out a table and chairs, or a bench, and plant a small garden. Without a soft edge, residents will not hang out there; and with no people, there's no chance to chat—and no chance to develop community.

**Front Side, Back Side.** Just as in many pocket neighborhoods, most dwellings in Danish cohousing developments have a public side and a private side. The kitchen and dining spaces are typically in front, where a parent can look out and see kids playing, see who's coming and going, or call out to a passing neighbor. The front side is social; the back side is private. When you're sitting outside the front door, the implied message is, "I'm open to chat"; while on the back patio, the message is, "This is my space, do not disturb."

The front side is social (below), while the back side is reserved for family and invited guests (above).

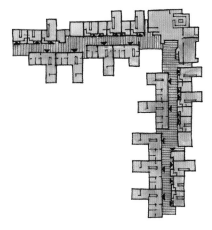

Taking the form of a pedestrian street a step further, the Jystrup community has a fully enclosed covered walkway with apartment units opening up to it—ideal for the long, rainy Danish winters.

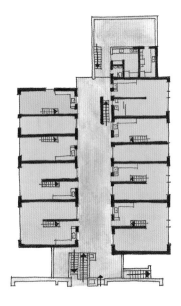

Drivhuset.

## Covered Pedestrian Street

The central commons at Jystrup (founded in 1984) takes the idea of the open pedestrian street a step further: In response to the long, dark Danish winters, it is a year-round, glass-covered pedestrian street. In a very real sense, the pedestrian street is an extension of the Common House, so everyone has daily contact here. As in the other plans, the back side opens to the private yard and shared woodland.

## Covered Atrium

Drivhuset, our last example (completed in 1984), is a renovated factory flanked on two sides by two-story units with the commons in the enclosed atrium. The covered space is wider than in Jystrup, which allows everyone to have a full dining table outside their apartments. Though it may be raining outside, adults are likely to be chatting over tea while kids are doing artwork. This is where unprogrammed, unscheduled activities happen; in short, this is where the community bonds.

# COHOUSING TAKES ROOT

Gudmand-Høyer's first attempt at cohousing was met with strong opposition from neighbors, who were apprehensive about collective housing nearby. Once cohousing communities were in place, however, they grew in popularity and became recognized as a viable housing form throughout Denmark. It is estimated that there are currently more than 1,000 cohousing communities in the country, housing about 1 percent of the Danish population. The cohousing model has taken root around the world as well, with examples throughout Europe, the United Kingdom, Australia, New Zealand, Japan, Canada, and the United States.

Drivhuset, which translates as "greenhouse," is a community that made its home in a renovated factory with a central covered atrium.

# NEIGHBORHOOD PIONEER

## JAN GUDMAND-HØYER

As a young Danish architecture student, Jan Gudmand-Høyer wrote a paper in 1951 on the collective live–work Kibbutz communities that were emerging in Israel. A short time after that, he read Thomas More's book *Utopia*, published in 1516, about an imaginary communal society with housing cooperatives of 30 families each, sharing meals and child care. These compelling ideas came into focus in his own designs as a graduate student at Harvard. Convinced of their virtues, Gudmand-Høyer worked tenaciously to build the first pioneering cohousing models with his friends and family, and he has given his entire career to establishing cohousing as a widely accepted housing option.

## CHAPTER 17

# Cohousing in America

Katy McCamant first came across cohousing as an architecture student in Denmark in 1980. As she describes the experience, "It seemed like such an obvious approach to housing that I assumed most American architects would already know about it. I assumed wrong." A few years later, she and her husband, architect Chuck Durrett, went back to Denmark for a closer look as they were pondering how to balance young careers and family life. Their visit expanded to more than a year of travel, study, and living

in a number of communities, and eventually to their book, *Cohousing: A Contemporary Approach to Housing Ourselves*. This book, and their work with helping design and develop dozens of cohousing communities in North America, fueled the cohousing movement in America.

While the cohousing model has achieved mainstream acceptance in northern Europe, this housing option asks residents to think cooperatively—a challenge to the dominant individualism of many Americans. Yet for an increasing number of people, this lifestyle choice is just what they have been looking for.

Cohousing residents take part in planning their community—from land acquisition and site and building planning to permitting, construction, and ongoing management.

## GETTING INVOLVED

A key tenet of cohousing is having residents involved in the planning process from the very beginning. Most people, however, know very little about development and construction, so the process can be daunting. Groups usually work with professional building consultants, but consultants without facilitation skills can find working with 40 clients to be intimidating.

McCamant and Durrett found they needed to become community organizers and facilitators, as well as architects, to realize their vision. They taught communication skills and decision-making techniques to new groups and helped them clarify housing goals, secure land, and coordinate with developers, government agencies, banks, and engineers. In the case

145

Nevada City Cohousing is a multigenerational intentional community—one of hundreds that have been built across America.

## WHAT MAKES A COMMON HOUSE WORK?

For cohousing residents, the commons must include a Common House where all can cook and share meals together. Its location in the community and the design of the building are critical to whether it gets used a lot or a little.

**Location.** The best spot for a Common House is at the focal point of daily comings and goings, typically between the parking area and the residences.

**In View.** When people can see activity happening, they'll likely feel encouraged to join in.

**Sunny Spot.** Locating a sunny outdoor area next to the Common House creates an inviting and pleasant place to be and helps weave indoor and outdoor activities.

**Key Activity Areas.** Besides the kitchen and dining room, incorporating areas such as a mail center, laundry facilities, a cooperative store, and a child-care room will promote daily use of the commons.

**Central Kitchen.** When the kitchen is at the crossroads (but not in the road), people will see and smell what's cooking, and the cooks will feel part of the community.

**Kids' Room.** Children make dinner a family affair, but it's best to have a separate room nearby where kids can play while the adults enjoy lingering conversations.

**Isolate the Cleanup.** After dinner, the noise of washing dishes can also be disruptive, so dishwashing should be located in a separate room.

**Acoustic Surfaces.** Covering major surfaces in the dining room with sound-absorbing material will limit the noise buildup and make dining with 60 others a more pleasurable experience.

**Lighting.** The lighting in the dining room must serve a variety of group functions, yet be intimate for dining. A good solution has adjustable fixtures that drop low over every table, creating a focused and intimate pool of light.

146

The dining hall in the Common House serves many purposes: It can be a yoga studio, a performance space for a talent show, or a workshop for kids.

of Nevada City Cohousing in California, they went a step further. After seeing six different start-up groups come and go with no results over a period of 13 years, they made a decision to move to the area and initiate a group themselves. Out of a process they began in 2002 grew a cohousing community of 34 households, including 50 adults and 22 children.

## The Common House

The hub of all cohousing communities is the Common House. At 4,000 sq. ft., Nevada City's Common House is an ample and multi-faceted space for the community. It features a large dining room (with room for all residents), a commercial kitchen, a sitting room, kids' rooms, guest rooms, a music room, a mail center, and laundry facilities. "In the morning, you might find me with a couple of my neighbors gathered around a table with the paper and coffee," says one resident. "At other times, you might find a yoga class going on, or a sewing circle, music lesson, or clothing exchange. And some evenings, teens gather to work on homework, or watch a movie together." The main event, though, is the community dinner, served six evenings a week. It's optional, yet most households take part at least three nights a week.

Some Common Houses get very little use, whereas others are the center of community life. According to Durrett, "The best get 400 to 500 people-hours of use each week, while others garner only 100 hours."

The Common House is the focal center of Nevada City Cohousing. It's where the entire community gathers to eat meals together, pick up mail, and do laundry. Kids have playrooms, guests have a place to stay, and out front is a large swimming pool for all to cool off during hot summer days.

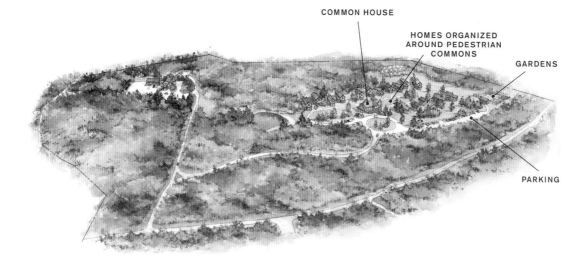

COMMON HOUSE

HOMES ORGANIZED
AROUND PEDESTRIAN
COMMONS

GARDENS

PARKING

Island Cohousing on Martha's
Vineyard was created as an
affordable housing alternative
for the island's workforce and
a model for clustered housing.
Sixteen houses and a collection of
common facilities were built on
15 percent of the 37-acre parcel—
preserving most of the land as
undeveloped open space.

# CREATING COMMUNITY, PRESERVING LAND

Rural areas are often battlegrounds for competing interests.
Developers want cheap land to be able to sell their homes at a lower
price point. Yet this gobbles up land in ways that spell s-p-r-a-w-l. So
planning commissioners limit development to low density, as in one
house per 5 acres. This in turn translates to cutting up large tracts with
roads and fences.

On Martha's Vineyard, an island off Massachusetts's southern shore,
these problems are intensified by stratospheric home prices and a fixed
boundary (the shore), creating a chronic shortage of affordable housing
for the island's workforce.

John Abrams, founder of a design/build firm on the island, saw
cohousing as a possible win–win solution. In the late 1990s, he
gathered a core group of potential residents and, with his own family,
worked to formulate goals and objectives, search for land, and design a
neighborhood. Finding inspiration in Danish cohousing, they developed
a plan for a 37-acre woodland parcel, including 7 acres for Abrams's
business. The plan, however, did not fit local zoning regulations.

In the collaborative spirit that Abrams runs his business, they
approached the planning commission not as adversaries, but as public
servants. "We saw their purpose as being the same as ours: to shape
a better community," Abrams explains. "So we came to them with a
project that anticipated their concerns." The commissioners responded
by working with them to improve the proposal and, in the end, not only
approved the project, but also changed the general zoning bylaws. To
which, Abrams quips, "Small stones can make big ripples."

To keep building costs down, customization was limited. All the building plans are variations of the same basic two-bedroom plan, with a kitchen and dining area opening to the living room. Options included hardwood cabinets, slate countertops, and adding bump-outs for additional bedrooms or a second bath.

## Creating Guidelines, Making Choices

Before jumping into a design, the group developed a six-page list of design objectives, including such guidelines as the following:

- Cluster houses tightly to preserve open space
- Make buildings simple, spare, and straightforward
- Build economically to allow for a diversity of households
- Plan for solar panels by providing at least 300 sq. ft. of south-facing roof
- Use salvaged and certified sustainably harvested lumber wherever possible
- Save as many existing trees as possible

These statements proved helpful when working out the details. It also helped to have models nearby. For example, one woman in the group couldn't imagine living closer than 100 ft. from another house. A visit to the nearby Oak Bluffs neighborhood (see p. 20) allowed the group to feel the effects of house spacing and layout, which helped them decide on how tight to cluster their homes. Now, the woman is delighted to live only 20 ft. away from her neighbor.

When some in the group wanted the houses to have dormers, the guidelines about simple shapes and planning for solar panels helped them come into consensus. Other choices were not as easy. Saving trees meant mapping them with a detailed survey and vigilantly protecting them from underground lines and pipes, construction pollution, and heavy trucks. "This complication probably cost about $100,000, but what kind of landscape replacement could we buy for that amount? Very little." The group made the choice, and now their houses nestle into the site like they've been there for decades.

With cars held to the perimeter, residents use carts to ferry groceries, gear, and even young children from the car door to the front door.

## LIVING IN COHOUSING

After a long day at work, it can be a relief to walk over to the Common House for a warm dinner with your family and friends. No shopping, no cooking, no cleanup. But what about those occasions when you want some alone time? Being in a noisy dining room with 40 others may not be a relief.

For many residents, it's a daily choice. One night you might be cooking dinner for eight families, but the next night you'd rather have leftovers in front of the television. Days can go by without engaging in community activities, but when something happens—you get sick, for example—it's comforting to know that your neighbors will come through with soup and a helping hand.

The level and intensity of community involvement varies from one group to another, and rarely are there rules for how much to be involved. It's more a matter of personal choice, and being tolerant of the choices others make.

Essentially, though, cohousing is a lifestyle that is all about community. It's about sharing, working, and making decisions together. The choice may not be for everyone, but for those who find that it's to their liking, there is nothing like it.

## CHAPTER 18

# Greening the Neighborhood

Half a world away, in Australia and New Zealand, two groups have taken the global environmental crisis to heart and built small-scale communities as templates for ecologically based cities. It is no surprise that their planning and design principles closely align with the key ideas of pocket neighborhoods, and that they are developed and organized using cohousing processes and social structures.

# EARTHSONG: A VISION COMES TO FRUITION

In the mid-1990s, Robin Allison, an architect from Auckland, called a group together to create New Zealand's first cohousing community, Earthsong Eco-Neighborhood. Their founding vision had three components: sustainable design and construction, respectful and cooperative community, and education by demonstration.

Earthsong is home to nearly 70 residents—including young families, singles, and seniors—residing on just over 3 acres in a suburb outside of Auckland. The community is laid out with 32 homes in clusters of two- and three-story dwellings arranged along common paths and shared courtyards. Dwelling types range from one-bedroom studios to four-bedroom houses, to accommodate a wide range of ages and household types.

Accessibility for older or less mobile people was an important factor in the design of the homes, as well as the site. Seven of the houses were built to accommodate residents with limited mobility, and all buildings have level-entry thresholds to their ground floor area. Exterior pathways are limited to a 1:20 slope, extending full access throughout the site to all.

Children's needs are accommodated, too. In addition to young child and teen rooms in the Common House, there's a car-free central courtyard, with a playhouse, large sandpit, and children's vegetable garden. Parents and neighboring friends take turns supervising a childcare group, as well as offering watchful eyes and welcoming kitchens for their young friends. Cars and parking are limited to a portion of the site, allowing the area around all of the houses to be car-free. The exception is the central path for emergency vehicles and heavy deliveries.

As with other cohousing communities, residents share extensive common facilities. At the hub of the Earthsong neighborhood, near the main entry and parking area, is the Common House, which includes a kitchen and dining space for community dinners, children's room, and shared laundry. Nearby is a shared workshop for small woodworking projects and bike repair. And at the back of the site, next to the pond, is the community food garden and orchards. The front portion of the site is reserved for the development of small businesses and shops that will enhance the adjacent commercial center and provide work opportunities for both Earthsong residents and the wider community.

The temperate climate of New Zealand's North Island is ideal for bananas, oranges, lemons, and peaches. It is also where the inspiration for an ecologically based community has come to fruition.

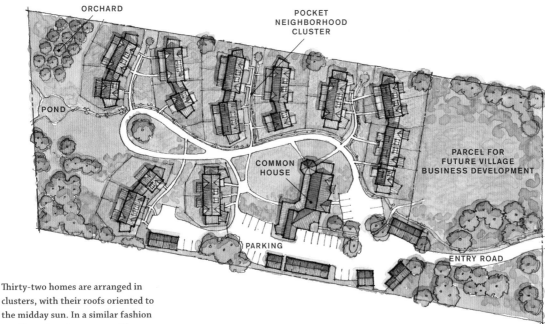

ORCHARD

POCKET
NEIGHBORHOOD
CLUSTER

POND

PARCEL FOR
FUTURE VILLAGE
BUSINESS DEVELOPMENT

COMMON
HOUSE

PARKING

ENTRY ROAD

Thirty-two homes are arranged in clusters, with their roofs oriented to the midday sun. In a similar fashion as other cohousing communities, parking is held close to the periphery, with residents and guests walking past a centrally located Common House to their front doors. At the front of the site, near the entry road, is a parcel being held for businesses and shops that support the local community.

Many of the mature fruit trees from the original orchard were retained, providing continuity with the history of the site, as well as an annual harvest for residents.

## Eco Choices

"Throughout the process, we made decisions in light of social and environmental criteria," reports Allison. Buildings face the northern midday sun for maximum solar exposure, passively heating concrete floors and actively heating hot water collectors on the roof—resulting in homes whose energy use is less than half the national average. Rainwater from the roofs is directed into tanks and used within the houses for bathing, washing, and toilets. Storm water flows into planted swales to encourage maximum percolation into the ground.

Top: Earthsong follows other cohousing communities, with its Common House positioned at the hub of the neighborhood.

Above: The covered outdoor room just off the Common House offers welcome shade from the sun and shelter from tropical rain showers.

Rainwater is collected from roofs for use within the houses. Overflow is directed into planted swales at the edges of the walkways to percolate into the ground on its way into a pond at the lower end of the site.

The group considered the impact of every material before making a choice, paying attention to issues such as embodied energy, toxicity, durability, and recyclability. Walls are made of rammed earth, a technique of compressing soil and sand between removable panels, providing thermal mass to the homes with a solid, timeless feel. Natural wood beams, cabinets, and interior surfaces are finished with nontoxic oils and paints.

Everything remotely reusable from the two existing outbuildings on the site was salvaged and reused as flooring, timber framing, furniture, and even a subbase for the driveway. Waste during construction was minimized by largely avoiding composite materials and by separating out reusable or recyclable materials from waste going to a landfill.

## Eco Education

Earthsong monitors the ongoing energy and water use of its buildings to establish the effectiveness of these systems, and shares this information with local and national organizations. It also set up an education program to assist homeowners, builders, and governmental organizations in learning about sustainability issues and methods—offering more than 80 courses and tours each year. In addition, Earthsong has been a catalyst in the local community for implementing neighborhood-scale environmental and economic-development programs.

The joke in cohousing circles is that it's the longest running, most expensive personal-growth workshop you will ever sign up for—but you get a house thrown in as a bonus.

Cohousing is known for its lengthy group meetings to work out decisions on everything from choosing a building site to locating a bunny hutch. Not all of these decisions are hashed out by the whole group—there are small group committees to do that (more meetings)—but all key decisions and policies go through a structured consensus process. Issues are stated; each person's information, opinions, and ideas are considered; and the group develops a thought-out solution. The final decision may not be everyone's first choice, but each feels heard and respects the decision that is made.

Earthsong uses a system of colored cards to speed up and ease the consensus process. Members are given a set of green, yellow, and red cards to hold up during a meeting. A green card indicates agreement; a yellow card signals that a person has a question, answer, or comment; and a red card either says, "Stop! We've gotten off-track! Let's refocus!" or "I disagree with the proposal and will block consensus." But there's a catch to blocking: If

"In the beginning I just wanted to get done with the meetings; now I value them for providing insight into the thinking and perspectives of my neighbors."
—Earthsong resident

someone red-cards a decision, they must work with others to craft a solution that satisfies everyone. After all this, if mutual agreement is still not found, the group can take a vote. "That's only happened twice in all this time," says Allison. "It's a good process that leads to better, longer-lasting decisions. And, it strengthens the community."

A color card system allows a group to get a quick read on their relative consensus regarding an issue, interject a question, or get the discussion back on topic.

I AGREE!

I'VE GOT
A QUESTION, ANSWER,
OR COMMENT.

I DISAGREE!
OR WE'RE OFF-TRACK—
LET'S REFOCUS!

# CHRISTIE WALK: AN URBAN ECO-COMMUNITY

Around the time that Earthsong was forming in New Zealand, architect Paul Downton helped organize an international environmental conference in Australia. Al Gore, a U.S. senator at the time, addressed the participants, urging a thorough rethinking of how homes, towns, and cities can become environmentally sustainable and socially responsible. After the conference, Downton and a small group of dedicated activists took Gore's call to heart and set out to build a pilot project for sustainable living in the heart of Adelaide, Australia. Christie Walk was the result of a grassroots effort at what Downton calls, "the grainy level of community-inspired action."

When Christie Walk was finally completed in 2007, a pocket neighborhood of 27 dwellings was built on a half-acre urban plot, including two-story straw-bale houses, three-story townhouses, and a five-story apartment building. "We had to become developers and builders—whatever was needed to carry the project forward," says Downton. Volunteers mingled with tradespeople as each learned from the other. "It was an educational process for all involved."

158

Christie Walk tucks 27 dwellings onto a half-acre urban site in the center of Adelaide, Australia, with room for shared greenspace on the ground as well as on the roofs.

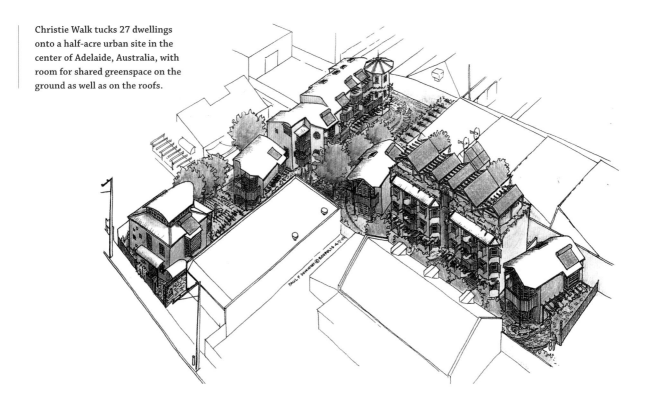

Even with more than 50 dwelling units per acre, there is room for shared open space—a treasured oasis in the city.

# NEIGHBORHOOD PIONEERS

## PAUL DOWNTON

Paul Downton has been pursuing ecological architecture and city-making since he discovered Frank Lloyd Wright's ideals of organic architecture at an early age. As an architect, urban planner, dedicated teacher, writer, and public speaker, Downton promotes the concept of "ecopolis": fitting human settlement into the living patterns of nature so that cities become places of ecological restoration as well as of economic activity.

Downton's firm, Ecopolis Architects, focuses on the environmental design of individual dwellings as well as planning for ecologically sustainable urban centers. He was a co-founder of Urban Ecology

Australia, a nonprofit environmental organization formed to actively promote people- and nature-friendly urban settlements.

## Building Responsibly

In a similar process as at Earthsong, the Christie Walk group engaged in lengthy discussions about what it meant to build responsibly, and then screened all their material choices by the following criteria:

- Nontoxic and nonallergenic
- Durability: longest life-cycle use, lowest life-cycle cost
- Lowest embodied energy: the amount of fossil fuel energy to manufacture, transport, and construct
- Sustainably harvested or recycled timber
- Consideration for future re-use and recyclability
- Preference for local and regional materials and services

Christie Walk packs a variety of environmentally sustainable features into its tight urban site. Its strategy for energy use and conservation combines passive design principles along with active solar collection, resulting in energy costs that are 50 to 90 percent lower than average. Windows are shaded from the hot summer sun and exposed to the winter sun where possible. All dwellings have solar hot water, and the roof of the apartment building is largely covered with photovoltaic panels. High thermal mass floors and interior walls separating apartments are combined with highly insulated exterior skins to buffer temperature swings. In the summer, the townhouses utilize "thermal chimneys" to draw cool air from the gardens up through the house to be expelled through vents in the roof.

Climbing plants and lush gardens soften and balance these tightly packed buildings. Here, too, there's an environmental message. The vines on the balconies serve a purpose: providing extra shade during summer, then dropping their leaves in winter and allowing more sunlight in to heat the dwellings. The entire roof of one building is covered in vegetation, offering a barrier against heat, edible landscaping, and a place for neighbors to gather (with a terrific view). Plants were selected for their low water use—a type of landscaping called "xeriscaping." In Adelaide's climate, water is precious, so every drop of rainwater falling on Christie Walk is collected and redirected to irrigate the gardens and flush toilets. All of these methods stem from permaculture principles, a design approach for human settlements and agriculture that mimics the synergistic relationships found in nature.

Above: Rooftops are fully utilized, with solar collectors, gardens for growing food, and a place to gather for an evening glass of wine.

Below: Climbing vines offer edible landscaping as well as shade from the summer sun.

## A Collective Effort

Christie Walk's environmental message may be the lead story, but its social story is no less compelling. The entire project came to fruition through the dedicated efforts of its residents, who actively participated in planning, research, design, and construction and are actively engaged in its ongoing operation and social life. This resident involvement, along with their shared common ground and facilities, is what defines Christie Walk as a cohousing community. But although many cohousing groups have formalized community participation, Christie Walk's system is more relaxed. Neighbors gather for communal meals every month or so, rather than several times a week. Community gardens are tended by those who enjoy the work—individually or at group "working bees" called as the need arises. "There is no pressure to participate," says one active resident. "That's their decision. We just feel they're missing out!"

"Rather than turning our backs on the urban environment and sprawling across the rural land," says Paul Downton, "we can transform cities into healthier places that are more energy-efficient, resource-conserving, productive, and respectful of the living world."

# CHAPTER 19

# Saging Communities

The first of 79 million Baby Boomers have just begun entering retirement. At each stage of their lives, this generation has questioned the status quo, and it's not likely to be different now. They are replacing the term "aging" with "saging" as a way of emphasizing the value offered by their years. Many are looking ahead and actively grappling with how to preserve independence without isolation. They are shunning the packaged leisure life of gated senior "communities"—which in actuality are for-profit business schemes—in a search for real communities that meet their needs. Cohousing fits the bill for many of these seniors.

Although most cohousing communities in America are multi-generational, there are currently hundreds of senior-only cohousing communities in Europe, and momentum is growing in the United States as the first pioneering communities become established.

The Silver Sage community in Boulder, Colorado, marks a trend toward seniors-only cohousing. The attraction for seniors is being proactive about their needs, and being around others who share similar interests and issues.

## ELDERSPIRIT

ElderSpirit in rural Abington, Virginia, was an early adopter when a group of former nuns and their friends built a 29-unit community for themselves in 2005. "We had no interest in becoming a 'leisureville,'" says founder Dene Peterson. "We are a community of mutual support and late-life spirituality." She and her neighbors have their own homes, gather for team-made community dinners, and offer care and companionship to one another. The community includes 13 privately owned attached homes and 16 affordable rental units laid out along a pedestrian path, with a Common House, prayer room, and shared greenspace at the center. As with other cohousing communities, residents and guests park to the side and walk through the commons to their homes.

# NEIGHBORHOOD PIONEERS

## DENE PETERSON

Dene Peterson is the driving force behind ElderSpirit. As a 75-year-old former Catholic nun, she saw her fellow former nuns aging, and considered their options. She was put off by the leisure-lifestyle pitch of mainstream retirement communities, but found inspiration in cohousing and in an article she read about spiritual community in later life. Highly motivated, she rallied others around the idea and moved forward on planning, financing, and building a community based on their needs and interests. ElderSpirit became the first seniors-only cohousing community in America and a model for others to follow.

## Why Just for Seniors?

Cohousing's attraction to seniors is not so much its active lifestyle, as it is its opportunity to be proactive about future living needs. Instead of waiting on family or institutions to set the terms of housing and care in their elder years, seniors are planning ahead for their needs themselves, and making choices that are accessible, manageable, and neighborhood-oriented.

The youthful vigor of multi-generational cohousing may be attractive to some seniors, but others prefer the company of those their own age, with time to engage in common interests and issues. It can be lonely for an elder surrounded by people focused on busy careers and raising families, and who are often gone during the day.

But isn't it a burden on healthy neighbors to care for those who are frail, especially if they are not so young themselves? Chuck Durrett, who introduced cohousing to America, says that it's always an individual choice. "But after building and living in a senior cohousing community, most want to help a neighbor in need—it's just what you do." ElderSpirit hired a care manager to help them, but Peterson is quick to point out that they are not a nursing home. "Should anyone need specialized care, we'd help find a long–term care facility and continue to offer our friendship."

> Residents of ElderSpirit planned a cohousing community for themselves around their needs, interests, and budget.

# SILVER SAGE

Jim Leach is a far-sighted developer who has built 20 cohousing communities in the western United States. While building the Wild Sage multi-generational cohousing community in Boulder, Colorado, he envisioned a senior cohousing cluster dovetailing with it on a site across the street. What surprised him was his wife's enthusiasm for the idea. She helped him loosen their roots to their home of 35 years and take part in creating the Silver Sage community with future neighbors.

Local architect Bryan Bowen worked with Chuck Durrett's office to design 16 dwelling units that met the group's desire for an environmentally responsive and socially engaging community. Completed in 2007, Silver Sage sits on a ¾-acre site nested within the larger New Urban neighborhood of Holiday, within walking distance of a grocery store, restaurants, offices, and the bus line. A series of attached two- and three-story buildings stretch the length of the block from east to west, opening to the sun with active and passive solar design features. Three duplexes counterbalance a courtyard, along with garages, a workshop, and storage buildings accessed off the alley. At the center of the community is a 5,000-sq.-ft. Common House with a full-size kitchen, dining area, media room, guest rooms, crafts, and performance areas.

Above: Silver Sage is a seniors-only cohousing community nested within the wider New Urban neighborhood of Holiday in Boulder, Colorado.

Above: Silver Sage brings together 16 south-facing dwelling units around a shared commons on a ¾-acre site.

## Living in a Senior Community

After living at Silver Sage for three years, Jim Leach describes his experience of community as "organic." Cooperatively managing affairs and activities requires effort and commitment, but he says there is a relaxed attitude about issues that arise. Whether that comes from being a seniors-only community is anyone's guess. Jim does venture, however, that "the health of a community stems directly from actively caring for it and for each other." He views it with an aspect that is almost spiritual—not in a religious sense, but experientially. "We do a lot together, culturally and intellectually. Someone reads a good book and tells others about it. We talk about politics and local activities. There is a lot to learn from one another and a lot of personal growth goes on. All this enriches your life as a senior."

The Common House is at the hub of the Silver Sage community.

# NEIGHBORHOOD PIONEERS

## JIM LEACH

If every developer were like Jim Leach, development would not get a bad rap. Jim has been at the forefront of green building and community-based housing for 30 years, and has consistently shown that making a profit and serving the common good can be parallel goals. Jim trained as an architect in the 1960s, but shifted to construction engineering and business as he realized his strengths and inclinations. He founded Wonderland Hill Development Company to put his ideas of affordable housing and environmentally responsible building into practice.

After being introduced to cohousing by Chuck Durrett and Katy McCamant in the mid-1980s, Jim recognized it as an ideal model for fostering community, and focused his efforts on helping prospective resident groups realize their dreams. His company is the largest developer of cohousing in the country, and he's often a consultant to other developers, generously sharing his hard-earned lessons and tools for building successful communities.

## A CAMP FOR LIFE-LONG CHILDREN

It started like so many close friends who've said, "Imagine us all growing old together!" Except in this case, these friends acted on their dream. In 1987, seven households bought 20 acres of rural land in Northern California, hired a renowned architect from Berkeley, and built a collective house to retire in. They named it Cheesecake Consortium, after the original Italian owners of the property, the Casatas, which loosely translates to "cheese pie."

Five members of the seven households trace their friendships to the early 1960s in southern California, where they organized a cooperative nursery school for their children. The families grew close as they vacationed together, saw their children off to college, and celebrated weddings, births, and deaths. "Our kids grew up together, knowing each other like cousins," says Jill Myers. "When we thought about retirement, we wanted this family sense of intimacy to continue, especially for our grandchildren."

All the buildings are raised up on stilts to be above the flood plain of a nearby stream. Although the building forms of the courtyard side are fixed, residents can opt to extend their apartments on the back side, expressed by accenting colors and materials.

Cheesecake Consortium began as an idea among friends as a place to retire. Seven households live together in four buildings that form a wide V around a sunny clearing in the forest.

The group imagined a kind of year-round summer camp, with an open invitation to their children's families and friends. Laura Hartman and David Kau of Fernau+Hartman Architects helped develop the camp theme into a design with informal and spirited buildings rather than standard-fare housing. Four colorful buildings—raised on stilts above the flood plain—form a wide V-shaped compound embracing a sunny clearing in the Redwood forest. Residents pass from one building to the next via connecting pergolas and covered walkways. Is this a hardship during inclement weather? "It's never been an issue," replies Myers. "If it's raining hard, we use the dash method!" During warm weather, living space expands out to covered porches for outdoor dining and overflow sleeping, complete with hooks for hammocks. And when grandkids and their friends come for the annual Camp Cheesecake, the broad steps that cascade from the deck make ideal seating to watch their talent show.

Four couples and three single women have their own apartments and share a common kitchen/dining/living area, library, and laundry-sewing room. Their private units each have a large bedroom, sitting room, and loft, but no kitchen. Dinners are shared in camp-style fashion, with

The wide covered porches of the Common House accommodate outdoor dining and chairs for conversation, and broad steps cascading down to the lawn make ideal seating for grandchildren's talent shows.

residents fending for breakfast and lunch on their own. The 15-ft. by 18-ft. common kitchen holds nine in a squeeze, working at a commercial-style stove, two sinks, counters, and baking area. A saddlebag eating nook and spacious pantry supplement the space. Although the kitchen is communal, no one is required to cook, or even eat with the group. "Those who like to cook, cook; those who only like to eat, eat," says one resident, adding the caveat, "but they have to clean up."

Contingencies have been considered for an elevator and ramps to allow for easier accessibility, but the group has not yet felt the need to act on these plans. Their first defense against infirmity is "being young at heart."

Meals are made in the compound's only kitchen. Breakfast and lunch are "on your own," whereas dinners are prepared by rotating cooking teams and served "sit down" to the whole family of friends.

"Imagine us all growing old together!"
—CHEESECAKE RESIDENT

# PART FOUR

# POCKET NEIGHBORHOODS IN EXISTING COMMUNITIES

**There's a lot to love about existing communities:** buildings of different ages that have been fussed with and fitted to meet the needs and expression of their occupants, canopies of mature trees that have grown to offer shade and scale, relationships that have developed from years of shared experiences. But like old clothes, communities can get frayed. They may not fit the way they used to or have the brightness of this season's fashion. So sometimes they are forgotten or passed on, left for those less fortunate to reuse.

It's tempting to leave it all behind and build new, from scratch. Big ideas can be laid out economically, with all the pieces where we want them to be. But what happens to yesterday's big idea that does not quite work? How can older communities, especially those built around the automobile, change to meet timeless and enduring needs for safety, sociability, and connection to nature?

Dozens of small projects initiated over time in existing communities can create a richness and fine-grained fabric

> "I see a commons in every neighborhood, and in every commons, neighbors coming together."
> —Mark Lakeman

not achievable in a brand-new community. The quirks and make-dos of infill projects may not be what a designer would create from a blank slate, but the character and color they bring add fresh life to a neighborhood.

The following examples highlight projects that bring nearby neighbors together, breathing new life into faded communities—stories of carrying a family's legacy forward, creating community in leftover urban environments, finding friendships over backyard fences, and reclaiming alleyways and street corners as safe nodes of neighborhood engagement.

## CHAPTER 20

# Infill in a First-Ring Suburb

In the 1950s and 1960s, the first rings of suburbs were being developed at the outer edges of American cities, where housing subdivision lots were typically ½ to ¾ acre in size. The production-built tract houses being constructed were small by current standards, for families with three or more children.

Fast forward to today. Land values close to the city are so high that these large lots are being further subdivided and built out with much larger houses—predictably with grand arched entries and two- or three-car garages. But this isn't the only option.

In a suburb near Seattle, a local jurisdiction passed a zoning ordinance in 1999 promoting cottage housing oriented around a courtyard. The goal was to provide more alternatives for smaller households—empty nesters, singles, families with one or two children—in ways that fit into the fabric of existing neighborhoods. The ordinance allows twice the number of dwellings on a parcel, as long as they are less than 1,000 sq. ft. in size, limited in height, face a central commons, and shield parked cars from the street.

Eight small cottages surrounding a courtyard tuck into the back of two suburban lots. This piece of land was originally going to be subdivided for a cul-de-sac, with four large, garage-fronted houses.

## A CLUSTER OF COTTAGES

Working within this ordinance, Jim Soules, Linda Pruitt, and I developed the back of two adjacent parcels with 8 cottages and a Commons Building around a central garden. The cottages range from 768 sq. ft. to 998 sq. ft. and were designed to be primary homes for one to three people. Though small by conventional thinking, they are made to live large.

Our plan has an access lane slipping between the two original front houses. The first view upon driving in is of the gable of the Commons Building, with rooftops of the cottages peaking up behind; garages are downplayed by their placement to the side. The resulting pocket neighborhood tucks into the surrounding neighborhood with little impact, and first-time visitors are often surprised by this secret discovery of garden cottages.

Above: The first view from the access drive is of the gable of the Commons Building (at right), rather than a wall of garage doors. The rooftops of the colorful cottages and the narrow end of the garages peak up behind.

Right: Before the homes were sold, the exterior color palette of the cottages was selected and the commons area landscaping was put in. Buyers designed and installed their own private yard landscaping, giving each home its own personal flavor.

174

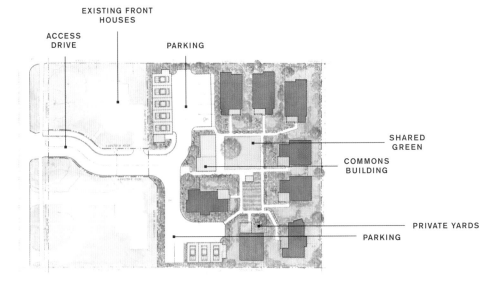

EXISTING FRONT
HOUSES

ACCESS
DRIVE

PARKING

SHARED
GREEN

COMMONS
BUILDING

PRIVATE YARDS

PARKING

Eight cottages and a Commons Building enclose a shared community green, with garages and parking clustered off to the side. An access drive slips between the two existing residences in front.

The patterns for the site and buildings followed many of the design keys noted elsewhere in this book. One of the essential patterns is a layering of personal space from public to private. Here, for example, there's a sequence of five layers from the sidewalk to the front door.

The houses and site were designed in detail, down to the palette of colors for all of the cottages and the paving patterns in the sidewalks. With help from skilled garden designers, planting in all of the common areas was put in before the homes went on the market. After moving in, owners created their own personal gardens, giving each a unique flavor.

The design patterns for the site and buildings followed many of those used at the Third Street Cottages (see pp. 60–71) and were focused on fostering a sense of community among residents. Major patterns included corralling the cars, walking through the commons from the car door to the front door, creating a sequence of layers from public to private, nesting the houses to ensure privacy between neighbors, orienting active interior rooms toward the commons to have watching eyes on the shared space, creating a Commons Building, and including a quiet lawn at the center.

At less than 1,000 sq. ft., the cottages may appear small, but tall ceilings, ample natural light, efficient floor plans, and plentiful built-ins make the petite homes feel and live much larger.

## COMMUNITY BY DESIGN

Among advocates of cohousing (see p. 135), it is considered a requirement that future residents be involved in planning and helping build their homes. This early participation is deemed essential for addressing their needs, desires, and priorities, and for building a strong sense of community.

However, not everyone wants to go through the years of work required by this endeavor. We took the initiative as designers and developers to do this work on our own, trusting our best judgment and hunches about the needs of our buyers, and how the design might support a sense of community once they moved in. Several years into living in this cluster of cottages, its residents appear to have a healthy, vibrant community. Did the design patterns contribute to that, or did the residents themselves have a natural propensity to get along? Or did other elements factor in? I believe the answer is, "All of the above." The design patterns seem to be effective, whether planned by the residents or not. Humans are gregarious by nature and, given the opportunity, will socialize. We also need some degree of personal space. Good design can achieve a balance between the two.

Resident Eileen McMackin describes her experience living with nested houses: "We live close together, yet it feels very private. I can see who's out in the commons, but I can't look into the house next door." Her neighbor, Darlene Feikema, talks about public-to-private layering: "If I want to be social, I just step out onto my porch. Yet if I'm engrossed in a book, I'll be left alone. The layering makes the boundaries more apparent."

It's clear, though, that a healthy, functioning community takes more than having good design patterns in place. Jan Gudmand-Høyer, who originated cohousing in Denmark, believes that sharing meals, physical work, and making collective decisions are all contributing factors. We found this to be true.

> Humans are gregarious by nature and, given the opportunity, will socialize.

Neighbors naturally gather to chat, yet the layers of personal space help make it clear when they'd like to be left alone.

Very early on in this cottage community, the first buyers gathered on Saturday evenings for a potluck—a tradition that continues today, with nearly all residents participating. Even though they see one another coming and going through the commons, the rhythm of a weekly meal makes it easy to keep their relationships active and alive. "Occasional ruffles are bound to arise, as in any group," says McMackin. "But our weekly potlucks and work together in the garden have helped form bonds that bridge the inevitable differences."

Feikema thinks of her neighbors more like a surrogate family. When her son Ben was 13 years old, her work called her out of state for a few days. As a single mom, she gave Ben a choice: Stay with a friend's family, or stay at home. "In my old house, I wouldn't have left him alone, but here I knew he had seven neighbors to run to in a minute if he had a problem. And I knew they'd look out for him." Ben stayed at home. The responsibility gave him a marked jump in maturity and independence. As Feikema says, "Living here is like being in a great big house with a lot of people. There's always someone to call on."

Facing page: On Saturday evenings, neighbors pull out tables and chairs from the Commons Building, bring out their potluck dinner offerings, and enjoy sharing a meal and good conversation.

## LIVING LIGHTLY

In addition to design patterns focused on sociability, we made steps to build well-insulated, energy-efficient homes. These, in turn, attracted buyers who wanted to live with a lighter energy foot-print—as seen in the parking area, where half of the new owners drive hybrid cars. Mike Nelson, a spirited solar energy advocate, installed photovoltaic arrays on his roof, reducing his net energy use footprint to near zero. That inspired many of his neighbors to do the same.

# CHAPTER 21

# Urban Homesteads

Urban areas often have an abundance of marginal, obsolete properties. Left vacant, these can become targets of vandalism, drug deals, and other misadventures. On the positive side, they can also offer affordable opportunities for new residential communities near transit lines, employment, shops, and cultural activities. A single household might feel vulnerable in an urban environment like this, but living together in a pocket neighborhood of 10 to 30 households allows residents—including women, children, and seniors—to feel safe in an urban setting.

Their sense of security is strengthened by design patterns that foster social interaction and keep "watchful eyes" on the common areas.

# DOYLE STREET COMMUNITY

The building occupied by the Doyle Street Community in Emeryville, California, was originally a deserted warehouse on a scant ⅓-acre site in an industrial section of town. It is now home to 12 households, who live in apartments surrounding a shared courtyard.

Architects Chuck Durrett and Katy McCamant took lead roles in this project, not only in organizing the effort, but also in actually living there. "When we first sought people interested in being part of this community," remembers McCamant, "all we had to show was an empty warehouse in a 'questionable' neighborhood." The area was struggling with drugs and violence and spotted with deteriorating older homes and small industrial buildings. "Nevertheless, the idea of an urban community attracted a mix of singles, families, and elders who helped

A small group of urban pioneers transformed a deserted warehouse into a safe home and vibrant pocket neighborhood for a dozen families.

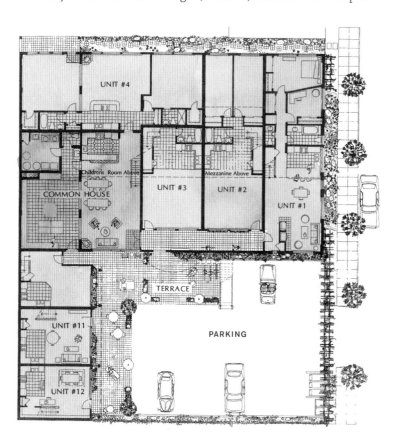

Twelve apartment units wrap around a parking court, which doubles as a play zone for children. Common facilities—including a community kitchen and dining area, children's playroom, rec room, and laundry—are located at the hinge of the L.

182

Top: The terrace off the second level provides a well-used space for families to get together for dinner, as well as an overlook to the parking court and street below.

Above: The original brick walls of the warehouse lend character to the common dining room and kitchen. As with the loft that was created above the kitchen, every space of the two-story structure is utilized.

us develop the design, champion the project through a tough planning approval process, and raise predevelopment funding."

The individual units, ranging in size from 780 sq. ft. to 1,600 sq. ft., reflect the character and personality of the original building, with its brick walls, corrugated metal siding, level changes, and large, multipaned industrial windows. The upper apartments take advantage of the vaulted ceiling and loft space to put every cubic foot to use. Terrace and patio spaces outside the apartments invite neighbors together for impromptu meals, card games, and conversation. On the ground level, at the hinge of the L, is the Common House—including kitchen and dining space for shared meals, a children's playroom, workshop, rec room, and laundry facilities.

> "A strong sense of community—not security gates—provides our safety."
> —Katy McCamant

## Watching Eyes

Security through "watching eyes" is built into the design. All private entries and most kitchens look onto the courtyard, and the Common House is visible to all who enter. McCamant, a mother with a young daughter, says, "I would not have felt safe living in one of the single-family homes in the area. But here we have a place that feels comfortable for single women, seniors, and families with small children—usually the most vulnerable in cities. A strong sense of community—not security gates—provides our safety."

## A STIMULUS FOR REINVIGORATING URBAN NEIGHBORHOODS

Pocket neighborhoods have a greater positive impact in urban settings than their size would suggest. Local issues are often discussed at community dinners and in daily conversations, and residents can easily coordinate to make sure they are well represented at public meetings. Their experience with group decision-making processes makes their voices especially effective in wider community decisions. And, given the type of person attracted to an urban pocket neighborhood, they are uncommonly active in civic affairs: volunteering for city committees, working to clean up local graffiti, organizing earthquake preparedness and safety programs, and planning neighborhood events. Because of these effects, city officials are welcoming pocket neighborhoods as a stimulus for stabilizing and reinvigorating neglected urban areas.

RETAIL | SWAN'S WAY ALLEY | APARTMENTS | OUTDOOR SHARED COMMONS | GARAGE | APARTMENTS

The cluster of apartments is on the second floor above shops, offices, a café, a children's museum, and a garage.

"We all have dreams about living in some kind of home. It's just not necessarily the one with a white picket fence."
—Resident

# SWAN'S MARKET

Tucked in the heart of a bustling commercial and cultural center in downtown Oakland, California, is a community of 37 people in 20 apartments clustered around a shared courtyard. This pocket neighborhood is located within a compound of structures called Swan's Market, named after a public market dating from 1917. The historic building covers an entire city block and includes a mix of small shops and offices, a crafts market, a café, a children's art museum, and galleries.

An understated gray gate off of a busy street belies the vibrant community found inside. Two rows of metal-clad apartments front onto a central pedestrian lane, open to the sky through a framework of structural roof trusses. This secluded space is a refuge from the city where residents take advantage of the ample light to plant gardens and grow flowers outside their red front doors. On warm nights they can be found using the community barbeque near the garden, enjoying Ethiopian food in the community room, or pursuing hobbies like coffee roasting inside the workshop.

Left: Swan's Market, a historic market building in downtown Oakland, California, made room in its renovation for a vibrant residential community.

Below: An open pedestrian street was carved out of the building, leaving the steel structure intact. The resulting space is a quiet refuge for its residents from the bustle of the city.

# BERKELEY COHOUSING COMMUNITY

A vacant and derelict urban lot with several run-down buildings was transformed into a pocket neighborhood community for 14 households.

Cohousing models can be effective in jump-starting an urban residential project. Berkeley Cohousing in California's Bay Area is one such example. This community began with a group of future residents acting on a shared dream. They bought a ¾-acre site with a number of run-down buildings on a busy thoroughfare and transformed it into a pocket neighborhood of 14 households and a Commons Building. The process involved working with the city to create a special ordinance allowing affordable residential ownership in the area.

Architects Durrett and McCamant worked with the group to come up with a plan to rehabilitate four existing dwellings and add four new dwellings. Individual units range in size and style—from small, 570-sq.-ft. Craftsman cottages to a renovated 950-sq.-ft. Mission-style house and a two-story 1,120-sq.-ft. shingled duplex—an eclectic mix held together by the central green. The group minimized the size of their homes to make them more affordable but also to allow for extensive common facilities.

The original "big house" on the property, a 1,600-sq.-ft. Craftsman bungalow, was renovated to become the Commons House, complete with a shared kitchen and dining area, living room, children's play

The ¾-acre site has a cluster of homes gathered around a central green, with parking clustered off of a busy street.

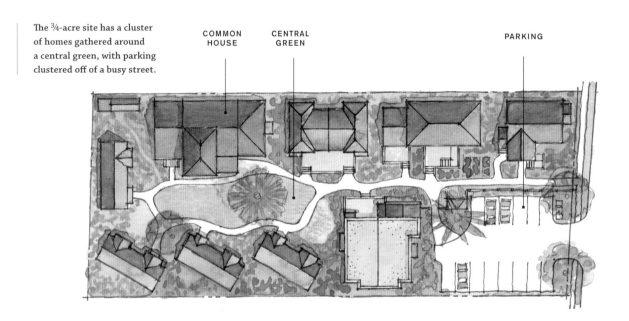

COMMON HOUSE    CENTRAL GREEN    PARKING

room, office, and laundry facilities. A guest room for general use is also included, reducing the need for space in each private home.

The cluster of homes focuses on a central lawn anchored with a mature Norfolk pine, which children make full use of before and after community dinners. Along the walkway, in a spot with full sun, is the community garden, supplying vegetables year round. Access into the shared commons is through a gate from a common parking lot off the street.

Environmental concerns were a high priority for the group from the outset. Indoor air quality and ongoing energy costs were considered in light of a tight construction budget, and priority was given to use of no/low-toxic materials, passive solar design techniques, and efficient heating systems. A number of residents have chosen to "go carless," taking advantage of easy access to community transit, car-pooling, and Berkeley's "Zipcar" car-sharing membership program.

Four new buildings were added to the four existing buildings on the site, creating an eclectic mix of styles.

Community residents come together several times a week to share evening meals in the dining room of the Common House. Salvaged redwood paneling and trim was restored to give this room its warm feel.

## CHAPTER 22

# Cultivating Community in the Garden

If pocket neighborhoods are all about nearby neighbors caring for a shared commons, then community gardens fit the bill. Neighbors within close walking distance of a shared plot of ground come together to plan, plant, tend, harvest, and celebrate their bounty. In working side by side, they get to know and learn from one another, and form long-term friendships.

# PERALTA COMMUNITY GARDEN

In North Berkeley, California, a thriving community garden brings together neighbors on land owned by the Bay Area Rapid Transit (BART). The oddly shaped parcel, perched directly over a transit tunnel entrance, had been fenced off for years with barbed wire, accumulating weeds, broken bottles, and debris. Karl Linn, a landscape architect and community activist, spotted the property and enlisted the support of a city councilwoman to negotiate a deal to lease the land and find seed money for the project.

Neighbors came forward to clean up the debris and take part in planning the garden. When the design was complete, a wider network of volunteers stepped in to do the heavy labor. Teams of AmeriCore volunteers constructed raised planting beds, and installed crushed stone pathways and an irrigation system. The city recycling operation delivered five truckloads of compost, and local contractors donated equipment to spread and till the soil.

> "Once a commons has been built, it is animated and reanimated through daily use and care of the space, as well as by periodic rituals and celebrations."
> —KARL LINN

189

From the beginning of the process, artists were invited to include "works of art that intermingled with lush vegetation" and to help create the garden itself as art. At the center of the garden, artists and volunteer assistants created a large, mosaic-covered circular bench, often used for meetings and workshops by neighbors and local organizations. Other artistic projects include a Sunflower Gate at the garden's entrance, a mural made of stone pieces, a garden shrine fashioned from salvaged materials, and a Bird Depot—a 20-ft.-tall tower of nest materials for birds to salvage. Even practical projects like the tool and resource shed have been built with an artistic eye, in this case as a backdrop for paintings.

# NEIGHBORHOOD PIONEERS

## KARL LINN

Karl Linn (1923–2005) had a passion for building community from the ground up, rallying, inspiring, and working alongside local residents, students, volunteer professionals, artists, and youth service teams in designing and building gardens and gathering spaces. He recognized that when people came together to transform derelict urban lots, they also built relationships with one another.

A landscape architect, child psychologist, educator, and community activist, Linn pioneered community design centers and community gardens across the country. He grew up on his family's fruit tree farm in Germany and fled with his family in 1934 to Palestine, where he studied agriculture, started an elementary school gardening program, and helped create a kibbutz. He began a career as a landscape architect in the United States after World War II but was increasingly disturbed by the isolation of nuclear families in wealthy suburbs. In the 1950s and 1960s, he taught landscape architecture at the University of Pennsylvania, focusing on small-scale neighborhood environments and the relationships between people and their surroundings. He would take his students to inner-city

neighborhoods where they worked side by side with residents, designing and building parks, playgrounds, and community gathering spaces on vacant lots—much like his experience collaboratively building a kibbutz as a young man.

For over 40 years, Linn worked with a social conscience to guide the transformation of neglected settings into vibrant community spaces. "The essence of my work," Linn told a Sierra Club writer, "is awakening the commons and the spirit of community. For me, this kind of spirit is the basis for democracy—it encourages vital neighborhoods."

The garden has become a vibrant commons for the community, drawing neighbors together on a daily and weekly basis to grow food and gather for meetings, workshops, potlucks, and celebrations.

Linn envisioned this and other neighborhood commons as the basis for enriching lives and strengthening community. "These cared-for commons," Linn wrote, "function as an extension of home territory where neighbors meet casually as part of their daily lives and forge bonds of trust and interdependence."

Local "food resiliency" gardens bring nearby neighbors together to cultivate food and community.

# COMMUNITY GARDENS TAKE ROOT

Like the "Victory Gardens" of World War II, food resiliency and sustainability groups have been planting gardens across the country in recent years. These initiatives may start around efforts to grow local, organic food, but the efforts are also yielding friendships and a strong sense of community among neighbors.

In Port Townsend, Washington, the Food Resiliency Action Committee has been promoting the idea. "When we began our initiative, there were 3 shared gardens," reports Judy Alexander, director of the program. "Now there are 25. Neighbors have been transforming vacant lots into abundant gardens serving up an array of fruits and vegetables."

The committee acts as a matchmaker, linking gardeners with each other and with nearby landowners who can offer space, and then following up by helping to arrange garden plot agreements. To assist groups in connecting and learning from one another, they set up a communications and networking website. Supportive hardware and gardening suppliers stepped in to offer significant discounts to garden groups on purchases such as deer fencing, water system components, potting soil, and tools. The state university's Master Gardener program also joined in, offering composting, soil preparation, and food preservation workshops, and cash grants for setup materials.

While all the neighborhood gardens are part of a wider community network, each group figures out its own structure and makes its own decisions. Most choose to organize as community gardens, rather than as a pea-patch with individual plots. The advantage is that neighbors work together as a group, and in so doing establish a group bond.

In a community garden, a diverse group of people can bring a range of gifts and talents to bear on a project. And at the end of all their work is often a harvest dinner.

# CHAPTER 23

# Taking Down the Fences

It's a fact of life that many of us don't know our neighbors very well. One way to get to know them better is to invite them over for coffee now and then or to arrange neighborhood potlucks and street parties. A less conventional (but equally or more effective) option is to take down the fences dividing the properties and begin sharing the joined backyards.

# N STREET COHOUSING

Two neighbors in a subdivision of ranch houses in Davis, California, decided to take out the fence between their properties. Adjacent households joined the fold and the group began to define themselves as a community. They shared several meals a week, planted a community garden, and used consensus decision-making procedures for shared concerns, similar to those described in Chapter 18.

Eventually the residents of the ranch-house subdivision adopted the cohousing model as a guide and gave themselves a name: "N Street Cohousing." Excitement grew each time a new house on the periphery joined in. "Fence Tearing Down Parties" became an institution. The combined backyards of 18 houses now span almost the entire center of the block—a community of 50 adults and 14 children.

Kevin Wolf, the original founder of N Street, is clearly a cheerleader for the advantages of shared backyards. But he understands that taking down fences can raise a neighbor's anxiety level. "So we take care to dismantle and save the old fence's wood. If things don't work out, they can easily put the fence back up." Even though the fences have been removed, none of the property lines have been adjusted. As far as the city and the bank are concerned, these are detached, single-family dwellings. Each household owns or rents its property separately. The culture, though, tends toward communal.

When a new property is added to the community, there are only two conditions attached: the meandering flagstone pathway that connects the neighbors must extend across the property. And, there must be some element created by the new members that benefits the community, such as a shared vegetable garden, chicken coop, children's playhouse, hot tub, or beehives (yes, this is true).

Kevin Wolf has been shepherding the removal of his neighbors' fences over a period of more than two decades, while fostering a vision of community with his engaging and generous spirit.

193

COMMON HOUSE

LAWN

GARDEN

Taking the fences down behind 18 houses and duplexes created a central commons shared by all. None of this is apparent from the street, nor from the city tax surveys that show no change in the underlying property lines.

## COMMUNITY TRADITIONS

In a community, success hinges not on what is received, but on what is given. N Street resident Linda Cloud considers one of her biggest contributions to be helping create traditions, like the annual gift exchange (with the Donny Osmond record that keeps reappearing every year), the backyard Easter egg hunt and brunch, and the summer camping trip. "The gift of sharing these experiences, and the activities we share every day, is that my neighbors have become my closest friends."

A flagstone pathway links all the homes.

# TEMESCAL CREEK

By nature, every backyard neighborhood is unique, and each community has its own timetable. One may start with two or three families removing their fences and then waiting years before a neighboring property becomes available and a friend buys in. Another group of families may start with a vision of living collectively and then look for adjacent houses to buy together. Such is the case with five families who formed the Temescal Creek Cohousing group and purchased three adjacent 1920s duplexes in North Oakland, California. They had a vision of living together in a community, but rather than start from scratch, as most cohousing groups do, they chose to retrofit the old houses to meet their needs. The decision catapulted them into their homes in a matter of months. Their first project was taking down the fences. Then came planting beds for strawberries, tomatoes, and peas, and a play set for the kids.

The initial cluster of homes later expanded when three contiguous houses came on the market, and the community grew to 20 people, including 6 children and 3 renters. The opportunity allowed them to tear down an old three-car garage in a backyard and build a Common House

This backyard neighborhood began with five families purchasing three adjacent duplexes, and then taking down the fences to bring them together.

with an apartment on the upper level. The common kitchen and dining room came just in time, as the residents had outgrown sharing meals in each other's homes.

## Benefits of a Shared Backyard

The shared backyard arrangement gives everyone a larger yard, and opportunities to engage with neighbors on a daily, informal basis. But the backyard commons probably affects the lives of the children in the neighborhood more than the adults. They are free to run about, play ball, build forts, or join in a rally of foosball or ping-pong in the Common House. Best of all, there are usually other kids around to play with. At the same time, children develop close and caring relationships with adults other than their parents, seeing them as playmates, role models, and an occasional listening ear.

There are benefits for the parents, too, of course. They can be relaxed about safety issues in such a protected environment and with other adults looking on. And they can rely on neighbors to pick up the slack when they need help, whether it is childcare for young children or helping with homework.

Above: A shared backyard welcomes informal interaction among neighbors on a daily basis, adults and children alike.

Facing page: A new structure was built in the combined backyards to house a common kitchen and dining room on the ground level and an apartment upstairs.

Above and facing page (top): A group of friends purchased an apartment building in Cambridge, Massachusetts, together and transformed the backyard into a shared picnic and play area.

# CAMBRIDGE FRIENDS

"What really sold us on the building was the asphalt-covered back lot coming up with weeds," recalls Sue Stockard, thinking back 35 years to the time when she and her husband along with six friends were looking for an apartment building to buy together in Cambridge, Massachusetts. Each of the couples had young children, and their dream was to live in a place where their children had built-in playmates and adopted aunts and uncles.

"It was not a desirable location at all," Stockard goes on to describe, as she points out the busy intersection with a gas station and railroad tracks. "But we imagined reorienting the building to the back, and making

an attractive backyard." There were no fences to take down, but the group did take out enough asphalt to create a large play area with trees to climb and grass to kick soccer balls. Some of the asphalt was left for hard-court games, "And, oh yes, for some parking spots, too."

The backyard was completely safe, and the children were welcomed in any of the neighboring apartments like family. In fact, with nearly everyone's immediate relations living far away, this small clan of friends functioned like a surrogate extended family to one another, celebrating many holidays and birthdays together, going to each other's children's concerts and plays, and combining vacations to the country. They helped each other through important issues, and engaged in lively discussions about politics and the school board. The dynamic has changed since the children have grown, but the bonds of friendship remain.

## FENCE OR NO FENCE? WHAT IS BEST?

Straddling the property line between two houses, this sitting shelter has seating opening to either side.

Robert Frost's well-known saying, "good fences make good neighbors," comes from a poem that questions the need for fences. In rural areas, a good fence kept your cow and animals out of the neighbor's fields. In residential neighborhoods there are few cows, and all throughout the American Midwest are yards that never had fences. In California, it is common to see 6-ft.-tall fences that prevent neighbors from seeing each other. Fence, or no fence? What is best?

The examples in this chapter have shown neighbors coming together by removing fences. Here's an example with the opposite approach: two neighbors working together to build a fence on their common property line. In this case, the fence is a sitting shelter with a covered roof, with seating on either side opening to each yard. Above the seat is a vintage stained-glass panel that allows light, but limited views (see p. 108 for another view).

## CHAPTER 24

# Taking Back the Alley

Pocket neighborhoods have shared common areas at their heart. But in long-established urban areas, where are these commons to be found? Turns out, opportunities are abundant and as close as right beyond the backyard fence: in the alley. There are more than 900 miles of alleys in Los Angeles alone—enough to reach all the way to Portland, Oregon—and the 456 miles of alleys in Baltimore could stretch to Toronto. Most of these passageways are unnamed and unclaimed by bordering residents. Rather

than dismissing alleys as dark and often dangerous corridors used only for trash pickup and garage access, city officials, alley advocates, and residents are beginning to see their potential to bring neighbors together, make them safer, and improve the environment.

As an example, planners in the Calhoun neighborhood of Minneapolis are recognizing the importance of alley security. Their master plan for the neighborhood calls for residents who live along alleys to name their alleys as a first step in taking responsibility and shared ownership. The plan also encourages alley-oriented "granny-flats" (backyard accessory dwelling units) and lowering fences to create visual connections between living spaces and the alley.

In Los Angeles, Jennifer Wolch has been working on the Alleys Project with graduate students at the USC Center for Sustainable Cities. This initiative brings public agencies and community-based organizations into partnerships to conduct action-oriented research on alleys in the city of Los Angeles. "Alleys can serve a number of purposes," says Wolch. "When resurfaced with porous materials they help reduce stormwater runoff. When drought-tolerant shrubs and trees are planted alongside, they create welcome shade. And with proper lighting and neighbors looking on, they enhance community life and safety."

Resident Suzanne Simmons and her neighbors in South L.A. didn't wait for a city initiative. They had had it with strange cars driving through and drug deals being made, so they gated their alley and set up hibachi grills, picnic tables, and benches. As she describes it, "The alley is now a place where we get together for potlucks, baby showers, and book club meetings."

Residents backing onto this alley in Baltimore worked together to clean up the garbage, take down the fences, and create a shared commons.

201

"Everybody uses the alley now. It feels like one big backyard." —PATTERSON PARK RESIDENT

# GREENING THE ALLEY

In Baltimore, alley advocate Kate Herrod discovered that the city's charter prohibited claiming alleys for private use because of a state-mandated policy. So she and her group, Community Greens, along with assistance from the University of Maryland School of Law, went to the governor for support in changing the law.

Returning to City Hall with state legislation backing them up, Herrod and other supporters worked with the mayor and city council to pass a local ordinance allowing residents to gate and green their alleys. The ordinance sets a tall hurdle: 80 percent of the people on the alley block must grant permission for an alley greening project to move forward. If the neighborhood wants to gate their alley so that no vehicles are allowed to go through, a unanimous vote is required, and approval must be received from fire, police, and utilities officials.

## WHAT IS AN ALLEY?

This seems like a simple question, but as planners and surrounding residents step forward to revitalize alleys, the nature of the alley itself is being redefined.

An alley is typically thought of as a corridor used to access garages and refuse pickup behind a row of houses or apartments. Alleys are like the Cinderella sibling, taking driveways, garage doors, and garbage cans from the street out front and making the street prettier and friendlier for pedestrians. Because of their utilitarian nature, alleys are often seen as dirty and dangerous, so adjacent property owners put up tall fences for protection; but with no one looking on, they add to the problem of security.

New thinking reframes the definition of alleyways as a connection between neighbors, a quasi-private/public space that brings people together. To foster safer environments, planners are encouraging owners to lower fences to ensure there are eyes on the alley—bringing security and life to an otherwise service-oriented corridor. Going a step further, they are allowing live-above-the-garage apartments and backyard cottage accessory dwellings (sometimes called "granny-flats") to bring a 24-hour presence to alleys. Residents are rethinking alleyways as well, cultivating alley gardens, creating alley art, and building gazebos to celebrate alley life. The result is a safer place for kids to play and neighbors to get to know one another.

# NEIGHBORHOOD PIONEERS

## KATE HERROD AND ASHOKA COMMUNITY GREENS

Kate Herrod may have set out to make one alley safer, but her goal is to revitalize alleys and community common spaces in cities across the United States. She recognizes that although cities may lack parks and open spaces, they have an abundant resource of land close to everyone: street right-of-ways, alleys, empty lots, backyards, and schoolyards. Restoring these spaces as community greens can make neighborhoods safer and kindle a renewed sense of community.

Herrod worked with Bill Drayton, the founder of the Ashoka social change network, to set up a nonprofit organization named Community Greens. She and her associates bring residents, government leaders, and community groups together to develop incentives and policies that catalyze the

development of new urban commons. "Our goal is to operationalize systems change," says Herrod. "We create tools to enable citizens to convert dysfunctional alleys and underutilized backyards into functional and beautiful shared green spaces that are owned, managed, and enjoyed by the people who live around them."

Residents along an alley in the Patterson Park neighborhood stepped forward to test the initiative. "Their alley was intimidating," Herrod said. "Vandalism and drug use were rampant," so efforts for reclaiming the alley were focused on safety, not sociability.

A huge rally was held to gather agreement from every household and from city officials to close off the alley. They succeeded. Residents then worked together to clean up the garbage, take down the fences, and raise money to build a gate. They painted colorful planter pots, brought out picnic tables and lounge chairs, and celebrated with a crab feast. According to one neighbor, "I thought it was a great idea . . . but I didn't realize that it would be such a great community-building project." Follow-up surveys have reported that crime has been eliminated, adults enjoy a renewed sense of community, and parents feel safe about their children playing in the alley.

At this writing, three other alleys in Baltimore have been "gated and greened," and Community Greens is helping 70 neighborhood groups to process alley-restoration applications.

Residents on this alley in Baltimore came to unanimous agreement to "gate and green" their shared corridor.

## CHAPTER 25

# Taking Back the Street

In villages of the past, crossroads functioned as public plazas where people came together for trade and socializing. It is only in modern times that intersections have become the province of cars and trucks, with people pushed to the periphery. It was this kind of thought that sparked the first "intersection repair" in southeast Portland, Oregon. "We recognized that our houses were landlocked by busy streets," explains activist and designer Mark Lakeman. "All of it is public space, yet no one can use it!"

When a child was hit trying to cross the street, Lakeman and his neighbors presented an idea to the Department of Transportation to slow traffic and raise the livability of the neighborhood: They would paint, at

Neighbors surrounding a street
intersection in Portland, Oregon,
took it upon themselves to paint
a mandala on the pavement
as a way to slow traffic. This
"intersection repair" sparked a
resurgence of community building
projects throughout the city.

no cost, a 70-ft.-diameter mandala over the intersection. The department
turned them down, but the neighbors decided to follow through with
their plan anyway. "Imagine the response from Ed, our neighborhood
policeman, when he drives up to see 100 people, including little kids and
grandmothers, painting this huge circle," tells Lakeman, as he continues
the story. "We're standing there holding wet rollers, smiling at Ed.
Nobody's running away. He gets out of his car, looks around, and the only
thing he says is, 'I ain't touching this.' He backs away and drives off, and
never even reports us."

# THE INTERSECTION REPAIR ORDINANCE

Portland's City Council took up the matter in lively debate. In the end, the
mayor and council members recognized the power of such projects to build
strong neighborhoods, and legalized the process through an Intersection
Repair Ordinance applying to all of Portland's 96 neighborhoods. To paint
an intersection, 80 percent of
all residences within a two-
block radius must sign off on
the project. At this writing, 16
intersections have been painted.

> "Intersections—like old village plazas and
> piazzas—are where people come together.
> That's what we're trying to do here."
> —MARK LAKEMAN

Following the approval of the
ordinance, City Repair formed as a
citizen volunteer organization to
facilitate intersection repair and
other "place-making" projects. Every spring, the group coordinates a 10-day
"Village Building Convergence" that brings architects, builders, artists, and
neighbors together for concentrated work on neighborhood projects.

Humor and whimsy are clearly part of their strategy. On one corner is
the "24-Hour Tea Station," where neighbors keep a cupboard supplied with
a thermos of hot water, clean cups, teabags, and honey. On another block

Above: A corner shelter made of peeled branches and a mud-straw-cement mixture called cob offers a place to sit and to read about local events in the covered cabinet on the side.

Below: A front yard cob wall includes a bench on the sidewalk.

Right: A poetry window in front of a writer's house invites passersby to read a poem or write their own.

# NEIGHBORHOOD PIONEERS

## MARK LAKEMAN

Design is an essential tool of democracy. That notion is a core principle of Mark Lakeman's view of a healthy society. Raised by ardent modernists who believed that all problems have creative solutions, his parents instilled in him his duty as a citizen to take part in shaping the world.

As a young boy, Lakeman would ride to site meetings with his father, a city planner. "We'd show up in the car with an 'official' emblem on the side, like in the Batman shows, and I'd pronounce, 'We're with the City!'" As an adult, however, Lakeman realized that most bureaucrats were not creative, and leadership did not always have good ideas.

In the early 1990s, Lakeman lived with indigenous Mayan people in southern Mexico, where he experienced villagers coming together in the streets and market squares, and actively engaging in shaping public spaces. The contrast to his native Portland, Oregon, caused a culture shock on his return. "I came from a village where the commons was everywhere, but in my own neighborhood, no one was interacting." In response, Lakeman and a few friends constructed a 1,000-sq.-ft. "renegade teahouse" of recycled wood, plastic, and old windows in their backyard, and invited neighbors to potluck tea and desserts. The response was tremendous, with neighbors from several blocks around spilling onto the street. Clearly, the teahouse catalyzed the community's need for a commons. Lakeman helped found the nonprofit City Repair organization to promote neighborhood commons projects throughout the city, and started an architecture and planning firm, Communitecture, focused on community- and sustainability-oriented projects.

is a lending "library": a glass-door bookcase with a roof where neighbors exchange books. And in front of a writer's house stands a poetry window, where passersby are invited to read a poem or write their own. Nearby, a child's tile reads, "I wish tomato plants would grow through my window and into my mouth."

"What better way is there than beauty and fun to change minds and bring people together?", Lakeman asks. Apparently it works. Former Commissioner of Transportation Charlie Hales says of City Repair's work, "When you walk around these intersections, you get it. People are out talking to each other. Cars move more slowly. There's a sense that you are in a place, rather than just passing through one."

208

Above: A group of neighbors on Milwaukee Avenue in Minneapolis saved several blocks of houses from demolition, and eventually replaced the street with a pedestrian commons.

Below: Milwaukee Avenue, as it was in 1974.

## MILWAUKEE AVENUE BECOMES A COMMONS

Stepping back in time, in the early 1970s, the city of Minneapolis housing authority planned to demolish 70 percent of the houses in a 35-block area south of the downtown. It was an effort to "renew" the urban housing stock of an entire neighborhood that was in disrepair. A small group of neighbors living on Milwaukee Avenue recognized the historical significance and intrinsic charm of their houses and fought back. Their narrow street included an unusual number of brick-veneered houses built for German immigrant workers in the 1880s. Bob Roscoe, one of the residents who led the charge, said, "We eventually made an end-run around the City by secretly submitting our four-block district for placement on the National Register of Historic Places. And it worked!" The city was forced to protect the homes and assist in their restoration.

A nonprofit development company was established and worked with owners, who performed a substantial portion of the work themselves. Sweat equity became a way of life along the street, with "gutting parties," structural repairs, and restoration of ornamental detailing. Hard work brought the community together. "We were like an extended family," says Roscoe. In all, 98 properties were preserved.

Years later, the neighborhood organization went on to convince the city to replace the street with a pedestrian commons, complete with shade trees, lawn, and a children's playground where the intersection used to be. As the Chinese proverb says, perseverance furthers—that, along with generous amount of community spirit.

Residents of the neighborhood convinced the city of Minneapolis to vacate the street and create a landscaped commons with shade trees and a playground. The homes are accessed by car from rear alleyways.

## THE LAND ORDINANCE OF 1785

Why is it that so few towns and cities of the American West have a village green, town commons, plazas, or neighborhood parks? The culprit is the Land Ordinance of 1785.

After the Revolutionary War, the new federal government devised a way to pay off war debts through a system of surveying and selling the largely unmapped territory west of the original 13 colonies. As the Indians relinquished lands, government surveyors divided the territory into "townships," 6 miles square, which were subdivided into 36 "sections" of 1 square mile, or 640 acres each. These sections were numbered 1 through 36, with Section 16 reserved for a public school. Sections 8, 11, 26, and 29 were set aside for war veterans, with the remaining sections for sale to settlers and land speculators. Unfortunately, the founding fathers did not reserve land for civic use or public parks. Those that exist arose from the foresight and generosity of town founders.

| 36 | 30 | 24 | 18 | 12 | 6 |
|----|----|----|----|----|---|
| 35 | 29 | 23 | 17 | 11 | 5 |
| 34 | 28 | 22 | 16 | 10 | 4 |
| 33 | 27 | 21 | 15 | 9  | 3 |
| 32 | 26 | 20 | 14 | 8  | 2 |
| 31 | 25 | 19 | 13 | 7  | 1 |

## CUL-DE-SAC COMMONS

Cul-de-sacs are like pocket neighborhoods, in that a group of homes surrounds a central shared space with minimal traffic. They fall short, however, in that cul-de-sacs are planned primarily for cars and service access, not for people and socializing. Most houses have multiple garage doors facing the street with no active interior rooms looking out. The message is, "Cars live here, not people."

The neighbors around Chestnut Hill Lane, a cul-de-sac on the outskirts of Denver, did not let their imposing garage doors and formal entries get in the way of getting together. Several times during the summer they plan events in the cul-de-sac, taking over the street with lawn chairs, shade tents, and movable fire pits. Unplanned gatherings and block parties are just as likely to happen spontaneously when neighbors venture out to visit, sometimes with chairs and a dinner dish, or a glass of wine in hand.

**Cul-de-sacs are typically planned primarily for cars, and offer limited opportunities for socializing among neighbors (below left). Some communities, however, are taking the initiative to use the street for social gatherings (below right).**

Neighbors around this cul-de-sac regularly take over the streets for potlucks and parties. Rather than being off-limits for pedestrian use, the street is the space that draws neighbors together.

## Online Communities

Stephanie Smith, an architect and software designer in Los Angeles, had a similar idea to help cul-de-sac communities. She created an online application called WeCommune to help link needs and resources in a local community. The tool enables neighbors to organize potlucks and community projects, arrange childcare and carpooling, glean neighborhood fruit trees, and set up a buying club.

"The problem with suburbia," says Smith, "is that there is no culture of sharing." She makes a point that every household owns the same yard tools used only now and then: lawn mowers, weed whackers, wheelbarrows, rakes, and hammers. If a new tool is needed, the only option is to go out and buy it. Kids need watching while mom is out getting groceries? They have to go with her. The dog needs sitting while away on vacation? It goes to the pound. "What's missing is an easy and practical way to share resources and help each other," Smith explains. "WeCommune is all about bringing neighbors together around sharing resources, organizing community events and projects, exchanging services, and leveraging their combined numbers to buy in bulk." Households save money and energy, but most importantly, neighbors get to know one another and develop caring friendships.

"The problem with suburbia is that there is no culture of sharing."
—Stephanie Smith

## The Fabric of Community

As I finish writing this book, my wife and I are in the midst of helping our daughter find a house to buy. What we're finding is confirming the reality and significance of pocket neighborhoods. And in this process, we've experienced a synchronicity that has us smiling.

   We began our house hunting by narrowing the search to two or three old neighborhoods in Seattle that seemed the most walkable and the most livable. Soon we were perusing the real estate listings, comparing house descriptions, numbers of bedrooms, square footage, and prices. The information had us focusing on the attributes and amenities of individual houses. It was difficult to gather details on the qualities of local neighborhoods and the wider community beyond our online research about property values and proximity to schools, grocery stores, and parks.

   We toured the available listings, discovering that many of the houses that seemed spatial in the wide-angle photographs were actually tiny and awkwardly laid out. These issues, however, were not necessarily deal breakers, as long as we could imagine their potential for transformation. The homes we responded to most favorably were on streets where the houses seemed to have some relation to one another.

   Surprisingly, the one house that caught our eye was on a busy street with a bus stop just 20 ft. from the front door. It was the smallest house in the vicinity, but it appeared to have been cared for and loved. The backyard felt like an oasis with its trees and perennial flowers. When we walked through the back gate, we discovered an alley and a pea-patch garden two properties away. Suddenly, it clicked: we had stumbled upon what seemed like a pocket neighborhood, at least in potential. The end of the alley abutted a neighborhood park with a pedestrian path.

We could sense the connection among neighbors and a safe environment for young children to play in. In other words, many of the design keys I've been writing about in this book.

Going back the next day, we met some of the gardeners in the pea-patch. They said the garden was the result of local neighbors rallying the city to buy and tear down a dilapidated vacant house on the property. We also met the next-door neighbor to this property. She confirmed our sense of the connection among neighbors, and suggested the possibility of taking down the fence that divided the two front yards and building a common sound-buffering wall and gate to the busy street. Then we introduced ourselves to another neighbor on the alley who was dropping off his recycling. He said he was a writer and asked if I had heard of Sarah Susanka's book, *The Not So Big House*. "Yes," I replied. "In fact, two chapters of the book feature projects I've designed." His face flashed with a quizzical look. "Ross?"

"Marc?" Rushing into my consciousness from my memory banks, I recognized Marc Vassallo, who co-authored *Remodeling the Not So Big House* with Sarah. We hadn't seen each other in years, and I certainly didn't expect to meet him in a Seattle alley! He had moved to the Northwest two years ago with his family and had found a house in a great little neighborhood.

Marc's house faces onto the next street with the same pedestrian connection to the park. "This is definitely a pocket neighborhood," he said, describing how kids roam the block and neighbors get together for barbeques. Their current project is building raised garden beds in the meridian between the sidewalk and the street.

As we were exchanging stories in the alley, a man came along with his son in tow in a red wagon. They were en route to pick up some scrap wood offered by another neighbor to build a playhouse. Our conversation revealed stories of connections among neighbors within the surrounding three or four blocks.

My mind was spinning as I was hearing tangible, real-life details of all that I have been writing about. Simultaneously, a picture began forming in my mind that was like the Russian nesting dolls: individual houses with their own private yards, nested within pocket neighborhoods of homes on a block or alley, all within a larger sub-neighborhood bordered by busy city streets and a park. This community is in turn nested within a district within the city. It was a picture of a whole and healthy small-scale community within a large-scale world—not just an idea, but the real thing.

# RESOURCES

## Books

Alexander, Christopher, Sara Ishikawa and Murray Silverstein. *A Pattern Language: Towns, Buildings, Construction.* Berkeley, Calif.: Center for Environmental Structure, 1977.
*Here's the book to start with. An encyclopedic, yet easy-to-read study of what makes buildings, streets, and neighborhoods work—indeed, what makes environments human. Considered by many as the most important book on architecture and planning for decades.*

Alexander, Christopher. *The Nature of Order* (Volumes 1-4). Berkeley, Calif.: Center for Environmental Structure, 2001.
*Alexander's A Pattern Language was just the beginning. After 25 years of thinking about how the quality of "life" emerges in our world, he coalesced his theory into these four weighty volumes. It's dense, yet simple. Philosophical, yet practical.*

Beatley, Timothy. *Green Urbanism: Learning from European Cities.* Washington, D.C.: Island Press, 2000.
*A look at the sustainability movement in Europe with examples from 25 innovative European cities.*

Buchwald, Emilie (editor). *Toward the Livable City.* Minneapolis, Minn.: Milkweed Editions, 2003.
*A collection of thought-provoking essays by leading thinkers on how to create livable, sustainable cities.*

Christensen, Pia and Margaret O'Brien. *Children in the City: Home, Neighborhood and Community.* New York: Routledge, 2002.
*A colorful and diverse picture of children's life in urban environments.*

Christian, Diana Leafe. *Creating a Life Together: Practical Tools to Grow Ecovillages and Intentional Communities.* Gabriola Island, B.C., Canada: New Society Publishers, 2003.
*Practical information for establishing and sustaining intentional communities, including sections on interpersonal and leadership issues, decision-making methods, sample legal documents, and a profile of model communities.*

Congress for the New Urbanism. *Charter of the New Urbanism.* New York: McGraw-Hill, 1999.
*Twenty-seven essays expanding on the key principles of New Urbanism across all scales: region, city/town, district, neighborhood, block, and building.*

Corbett, Judy and Michael Corbett. *Designing Sustainable Communities: Learning from Village Homes.* Washington, D.C.: Island Press, 2000.
*Drawing extensively from the example of Village Homes in Davis, California, this book lays the ground for creating healthy, vibrant, and environmentally responsive new communities.*

Cullen, Gordon. *The Concise Townscape.* Woburn, Mass.: Architectural Press, 1996.
*A reissue of a classic book that should be on everyone's must-read list. Cullen's lovely drawings and clear text give language and understanding to the choreography of urban space. Why does this space feel so good? This book helps us understand this question.*

Duany, Andreas, Elizabeth Plater-Zyberk and Jeff Speck. *Suburban Nation: The Rise of Sprawl and the Decline of the American Dream.* New York: North Point Press, 2000.
*The city of the future turns out to be the old neighborhood. This book, by the founders of the New Urbanist movement, offers a critique of suburbia and guideposts for (re)creating vibrant, livable communities.*

Dunham-Jones, Ellen and June Williamson. *Retrofitting Suburbia: Urban Design Solutions for Redesigning Suburbs.* Hoboken, N.J.: John Wiley & Sons, 2009.
*A comprehensive guidebook for re-imagining outdated, low-density communities as sustainable, mixed-use spaces that reduce urban sprawl and the dependence on cars.*

Durrett, Charles. *The Senior Cohousing Handbook: A Community Approach to Independent Living.* Gabriola Island, B.C., Canada: New Society Publishers, 2009.
*A comprehensive guide to creating or joining a senior cohousing community, written by the United States' leader in the field.*

Durrett, Charles and Kathryn McCammant. *Cohousing: A Contemporary Approach to Housing Ourselves.* Berkeley, Calif.: Ten Speed Press, 1994.
*This is the book that launched cohousing in America; it is still the first go-to source about these communities.*

Farr, Douglas. *Sustainable Urbanism: Urban Design with Nature.* Hoboken, N.J.: John Wiley & Sons, 2008.
*This book knits together smart growth, New Urbanism, and green building—three movements that address the sliding scales of regions, neighborhoods, and buildings.*

Fosket, Jennifer and Laura Mamo. *Living Green: Communities That Sustain.* Gabriola Island, B.C., Canada: New Society Publishers, 2009.
*A good look at green communities thriving in America and the people who build them.*

Gehl, Jan. *Life Between Buildings: Using Public Space.* Copenhagen: Danish Architectural Press, 2008.
*First published in 1971, this book is still a perennial source for the way people use public spaces.*

Girling, Cynthia and Ronald Kellett. *Skinny Streets and Green Neighborhoods.* Washington, D.C.: Island Press, 2005.
*Good urban design and sound environmental design coincide in an examination of 18 green neighborhoods.*

Hayden, Delores. *Redesigning the American Dream: Gender, Housing, and Family Life.* New York: W. W. Norton & Company, 2002.
*A provocative critique of how American housing patterns impact private and public life.*

Jacobs, Jane. *The Death and Life of Great American Cities.* New York: Random House, 1961.
*One of the most influential planning books of the last 50 years, described as "the Rosetta Stone for how cites and neighborhoods work at a fine-grain level." Jacobs offers critiques of modernist planning policies, along with stories and insights for making vibrant neighborhoods.*

Katz, Peter. *The New Urbanism: Toward an Architecture of Community.* New York: McGraw-Hill, 1994.
*This was the first book on New Urbanism to focus a wide national conversation. It continues to educate and inspire planners and the general public alike about its key principles.*

Kellert, Steven, Judith M. Heerwagen and Martin L. Mador. *Biophilic Design: The Theory, Science and Practice of Bringing Buildings to Life.* Hoboken, N.J.: John Wiley & Sons, 2008.
*A scholarly yet engaging collection of essays on how we can design and build environments that integrate with nature and natural systems.*

Kunstler, James Howard. *The Geography of Nowhere: The Rise and Decline of America's Man-Made Landscape.* New York: Touchstone, 1994.
*A spirited, cutting review of the insanity of single-use suburbs by this angry prophet of American society. A good read, but one that should be coupled with a book about solutions.*

Langdon, Phillip. *A Better Place to Live: Reshaping the American Suburb.* Amherst, Mass.: University of Massachusetts Press, 1994.
*A critique of suburbs and an articulate introduction to New Urbanism, with clear perspectives on creating and repairing walkable, livable communities.*

Low, Thomas E. *Light Imprint Handbook: Integrating Sustainability and Community Design.* Washington, D.C.: Island Press, 2010 .
*This is a handbook for development and planning professionals to help build beautiful, livable communities with a lighter footprint.*

Mouzon, Stephen A. *The Original Green: Unlocking the Mystery of True Sustainability.* The New Urban Guild Foundation, 2010.
*A must-read book about "sustainability before the Thermostat Age"—common-sense, refreshing insights into how we can make sustainable places and buildings.*

Polyzoides, Stephanos, Roger Sherwood and James Tice. *Courtyard Housing in Los Angeles.* New York: Princeton Architectural Press, 1992.
*A jewel of a book documenting the typology and history of courtyard housing in Southern California.*

Register, Richard. *Ecocities: Rebuilding Cities in Balance with Nature.* Gabriola Island, B.C., Canada: New Society Publishers, 2006.
*This book is about rebuilding cities and towns based on ecological principles for long-term sustainability, cultural vitality, and the health of Earth's biosphere.*

Skenazy, Lenore. *Free Range Kids.* San Francisco, Calif.: Jossey-Bass, 2009.
*A humorous manifesto that encourages parents to let their kids be kids.*

Smart Growth Network and International City/County Management Association (ICMA). *Getting to Smart Growth,* Volumes I & II. Smart Growth Network, 2005.
*Two practical manuals with a wide variety of tools and policies to create diverse, livable communities. With case studies of successful projects and dozens of practical and financial tips.*

Southworth, Michael and Eran Ben-Joseph. *Streets and the Shaping of Towns and Cities.* Washington, D.C.: Island Press, 2003.
*The history and evolution of residential streets in the U.S. and Britain, with a critique of grid patterns and surprising arguments in favor of cul-de-sacs and shared streets.*

Stein, Clarence. *Toward New Towns for America.* Cambridge, Mass.: The MIT Press, 1966.
*A key book by an early proponent for Garden Cities in America, offering history, critique, and detailed descriptions—including pocket neighborhoods as building blocks for larger communities.*

Sucher, David. *City Comforts: How to Build an Urban Village.* Seattle, Wash.: City Comforts, Inc., 2003
*Filled with pictures and chunks of text, this little book is a series of modest, down-to-earth tips about how neighborhoods and urban settings can become more humane, human-scaled, and alive.*

Walljasper, Jay. *The Great Neighborhood Book.* Gabriola Island, B.C., Canada: New Society Publishers, 2007.
*Every page of this do-it-yourself guidebook is filled with examples, ideas, and resource connections that will inspire and energize citizens and local groups to revitalize their neighborhoods.*

White, William H. *The Social Life of Small Urban Spaces.* New York: Project for Public Spaces, 1980.
*This classic study of New York's plazas started a mini-revolution in urban planning. Through basic tools of observation and interviews, we can learn an immense amount about how to make our cities more livable.*

## Online Resources

**Ecovillages Newsletter**
*An informative newsletter about ecovillages and related projects worldwide.*
www.ecovillagenews.org

**Free Range Kids**
*A lively, informative blog about raising "safe, self-reliant children without going nuts with worry."*
http://freerangekids.wordpress.com

**New Urban News**
*Substantive, concise, and current information about New Urbanism, Smart Growth, and walkable communities. In print and online.*
www.newurbannetwork.com

**Smart Growth Network**
*An online resource tapping into the Smart Growth Network—a partnership of nonprofit and government organizations promoting development that boosts the economy, protects the environment, and enhances community vitality.*
www.smartgrowth.org

**the Original Green**
*Steve Mouzon's online resource and blog about common-sense sustainability and living traditions.*
www.originalgreen.org

## Organizations

**Ashoka's Community Greens**
*A nonprofit organization that empowers citizens to create and manage shared green spaces where people live and work.*
www.communitygreens.org

**City Repair Project**
*This group facilitates artistic and ecologically oriented placemaking in Portland, Oregon, through projects that honor the interconnection of human communities and the natural world. Their annual Village Building Convergence is a highlight.*
www.cityrepair.org

215

**Congress for the New Urbanism (CNU)**
*The organizational center for the New Urbanist movement; promoting walkable, mixed-use neighborhood developments, sustainable communities, and healthier living conditions.*
www.cnu.org

**Ecocity Builders**
*A nonprofit organization dedicated to reshaping cities for the long-term health of human and natural systems. They develop and implement policy, design, and educational tools and strategies.*
www.ecocitybuilders.org

**Global Ecovillage Network (GEN)**
*An umbrella organization for sustainable communities, initiatives, and ecologically minded individuals worldwide.*
http://gen.ecovillage.org

**International Network for Traditional Building, Architecture & Urbanism (INTBAU)**
*A worldwide network of individuals and institutions that design, make, maintain, study, or enjoy traditional building, architecture, and places.*
www.intbau.org

**Local Government Commission (LGC)**
*A nonprofit organization providing inspiration, technical assistance, and networking to local elected officials and community leaders who are working to create healthy, walkable, and resource-efficient communities.*
www.lgc.org

**Making Cities Livable**
*This international organization promotes livable, engaged, and sustainable communities through conferences, publishing, consulting, and networking.*
www.livablecities.org

**New Partners for Smart Growth**
*An annual conference bringing together leaders, advocates, and activists to confront the challenges to our built environment, and propose solutions for more livable, walkable, and healthier communities.*
www.newpartners.org

**Project for Public Spaces (PPS)**
*A nonprofit organization dedicated to helping people create and sustain public places that build stronger communities.*
www.pps.org

**The Cohousing Association of the United States**
*An active organization that promotes cohousing in America through conferences, workshops, tours, database directory, networking, and more.*
www.cohousing.org

**The Prince's Foundation for the Built Environment**
*Sponsored by the Prince of Wales, this organization has been working to reawaken living traditions that foster true sustainability and vibrant community.*
www.princes-foundation.org

**The Walkable and Livable Communities Institute, Inc.**
*With the passion of evangelists, this group is on a mission to make towns and cities throughout the world more walkable, bicycle- and transit-friendly, and livable. They work directly with community leaders, agencies, and organizations to transform urban spaces, block by block.*
www.walklive.org

**Walk Score**
*A web site that ranks 2,508 neighborhoods in the largest 40 U.S. cities on the basis of walking proximity to daily services and amenities.*
www.walkscore.com

216

# CREDITS

All photos and drawings are by Ross Chapin, except as noted.

FRONT MATTER

p. 5: Ken Gutmaker; Architect: Ross Chapin Architects (www.rosschapin.com); Developer: The Cottage Company (www.cottagecompany.com)

p. 6: courtesy Evelyn Duvall

p. 7: courtesy Deborah Koff-Chapin

p. 8: Architect: Ross Chapin Architects; Developer: The Cottage Company

p. 9 (left): Architect: Ross Chapin Architects; Builder: Kimball & Landis Construction

p. 9 (right): courtesy Wonderland Hill Development Co. (www.whdc.com)

p. 10 (top): Ken Gutmaker; Architect: McCamant & Durrett Architects (www.mccamant-durrett.com)

p. 10 (bottom): Ken Gutmaker; Architect: Ross Chapin Architects; Developer: The Cottage Company

p. 11 (top left): Architect: Ross Chapin Architects; Developer: The Cottage Company

p. 11 (top right, center): Ken Gutmaker; Architect: McCamant & Durrett Architects

p. 11 (bottom left): Robin Allison (www.earthsong.org.nz)

p. 12 (top left, top right, bottom left): Architect: Ross Chapin Architects; Developer: The Cottage Company

p. 13 (top): Architect: Wolff + Lyon Architects (www.wlarch.com)

p. 13 (bottom): Architect: Ross Chapin Architects; Developer: The Cottage Company

p. 15: from *English Villages*, by P. H. Ditchfield

p. 16: courtesy of the New York State Department of Transportation

p. 17: Architect: Ross Chapin Architects; Developer: The Cottage Company

CHAPTER 1

p. 21 (right), 22 (left): courtesy Martha's Vineyard Campground Meeting Association

CHAPTER 2

p. 26: Aleah Chapin

pp. 28-31: Architect: Alfred Tredway White

CHAPTER 3

pp. 32-35: Architect: Grosvenor Atterbury; Landscape Architect: Frederick Law Olmsted Jr.

p. 36 (top), 41 (top) 43 (bottom): from *Toward New Towns in America*, by Clarence S. Stein, MIT Press, 1957

p. 37: site plan by Ross Chapin, adapted from a drawing in *Toward New Towns in America*, MIT Press, 1957

CHAPTER 4

p. 45: courtesy City of Pasadena, Design and Historic Preservation

p. 46: drawings by Martha Garstang Hill

p. 48: courtesy Moule & Polyzoides Architects; Developer: Arthur Zwebell

p. 49: courtesy Eric Larson

p. 50: courtesy www.greatbuildings.com; Architect: Bernard Maybeck

p. 51: Dan Burden

CHAPTER 5

p. 52, 53 (bottom), 54-55, 56 (right): Ken Gutmaker

p. 53 (top right): courtesy John Kucher

CHAPTER 6

Architect: Ross Chapin Architects; Developer: The Cottage Company

p. 63, 64 (top), 68 (right), 70: Ken Gutmaker

p. 69 (left): Grey Crawford

CHAPTER 7

Architect: Ross Chapin Architects; Developer: The Cottage Company

p. 80: drawing by Martha Garstang Hill

CHAPTER 8

Architect: Ross Chapin Architects; Developer: The Cottage Company

CHAPTER 9

Architect: Wolff + Lyon Architects

p. 92, 93 (top), 94 (bottom), 95 (bottom): Mary Sweet

p. 93 (bottom): courtesy Wolff + Lyon Architects

CHAPTER 11

p. 102: Dan Burden

p. 103: Jerry Michalski, www.sociate.com

p. 105: Thomas J. Story

CHAPTER 12

Architect: Ross Chapin Architects; Developer: The Cottage Company

CHAPTER 13

p. 110: © 2005-2010 Sitephocus, LLC, www.sitephocus.com; Developer: Hedgewood (www.hedgewoodhomes.com)

p. 111 (top): Dan Burden

p. 111 (bottom): courtesy Bruce B. Tolar, Architect

p. 112 (top): courtesy Wolff + Lyon Architects

p. 112: drawing by Martha Garstang Hill

p. 112 (bottom), 114 (right): © Stephen A. Mouzon; Designer: Placemakers; Developer: Ed Welch, Dale Walker (www.thewatersal.com)

p. 113: courtesy Larry Duffy; Town Planners: Duany, Plater-Zyberk & Company (www.dpz.com); Developer: Whittaker Builders (www.newtownatstcharles.com)

pp. 115-116, 117 (top): courtesy Stephanos Polyzoides; Moule and Polyzoides, Architects and Urbanists (www.mparchitects.com)

p. 117 (bottom): © Paul Armstrong, Wiseacre Digital; Town Planners: Duany, Plater-Zyberk & Company

CHAPTER 14

Architect: Jeff Shelton (www.jeffsheltonarchitect.com); Builder: Dan Upton

p. 118, 120 (top): Cara Peace

p. 119 (right): © Bill Dewey

CHAPTER 15

Designers and Developers: Michael and Judy Corbett (www.michaelcorbettmasterbuilder.com)

p. 127 (bottom): courtesy Wayne Senville

p. 133: Architect: Ross Chapin Architects; Developer: The Cottage Company

218

# INDEX